America's Last
Steam Railroad

STEAM STEEL & STARS

Photographs by
O. WINSTON LINK

America's Last
Steam Railroad

STEAM STEEL & STARS

Photographs by
O. WINSTON LINK

Text by
TIM HENSLEY
Afterword by
THOMAS H. GARVER

HARRY N. ABRAMS, INC.
Publishers, New York

To my father and mother, Albert Link and Anne Winston Jones Link

Project Director: Robert Morton
Editor: Beverly Fazio
Designers: Joyce Rothschild and Doris Leath
Map: Doris Leath

Library of Congress Cataloging in Publication Data

Link, O. Winston, 1911—
   Steam, steel, and stars.

   1. Norfolk and Western Railway—Pictorial works.
I. Hensley, Tim.   II. Title.
TF25.N77L56   1984   385'.0975   83-14462
ISBN 0–8109–1645–2

Times Mirror Books

Printed and bound by Amilcare Pizzi, S.p.A., Milan, Italy

Frontispiece: Amazingly, the main line of the N&W's Pocahontas
Division actually bisects the business district of North Fork, West
Virginia. Here merchandise with Y6 No. 2197 in charge rumbles
down Main Street rattling windows and doors, but no one seems to
mind the intrusion as trains come through from the nearby coal
fields several times a day.

CONTENTS

On a crisp winter's evening more than a quarter of a century ago, a highly successful New York City photographer by the name of O. Winston Link was finding the nocturnal amusements in stately Staunton, Virginia, less than stimulating. On assignment from an advertising agency to a local manufacturer, he found time hanging heavy after a long day's work and decided to drive to nearby Waynesboro, where he knew the tracks of America's last totally steam railroad—the Norfolk and Western—passed through.

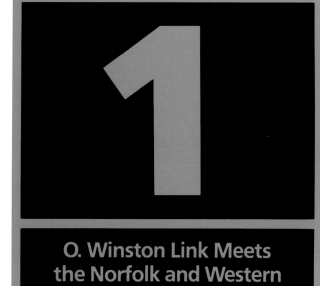

1

O. Winston Link Meets the Norfolk and Western

Seeking out local rail facilities was an avocation he had indulged since adolescence, when he would travel from his Brooklyn home to the Jersey City Terminal and Communipaw Yards, and one he continued to indulge as an adult, whenever he found time during assignments. Link had succumbed to the charms of the steam locomotive at a tender age, from the first time he saw a wooden toy likeness in a department store Christmas display. For, indeed, there is something fascinating about a steam locomotive—something almost animate and personal.

Left: Second 95, a southbound time freight, leaves the Waynesboro station in a spectacle of smoke and steam after stopping to make a set-off with Y6 2150. Agent F. C. Armentrout is silhouetted in the bay window.

Certainly the most aesthetic of man's mechanical creations, the steam train seemingly had a soul. It could sigh and hiss, clank and groan; emit impassioned shrieks and mournful toots; bellow and balk at hauling a heavy load or purr ecstatically as it romped the rails at more than a mile a minute, evoking a myriad of emotions associated with romance, mystery, adventure, loneliness, power, sorrow, and, somehow, comfort.

The iron horse seemed alive. Physical wants for fuel, water, and lubrication had to be satisfied before it would plow the rails. It commanded an army of men clambering over, under, on, or about it. And, like its thoroughbred equine counterpart, it had to be groomed and often coaxed and petted before it would perform.

But by the late 1950s, despite its charismatic qualities and well over a century of service that had tied the nation together in a web of wood and steel, the steam locomotive was rapidly disappearing from the American scene. Ever since the first successful use of the diesel-electric locomotive on the Central of New Jersey in 1925, the railroads had been converting to this more economical, though not necessarily more efficient, means of motive power.

In the years following World War II, "dieselization," as the modernizing was called, accelerated, and shiny new streamliners were initiated, in a last effort to salvage the passenger train. This was the twilight of the rail industry's golden years, before such entities as Penn Central and Rock Island would tarnish a lustrous image and paint instead a picture of decay.

By 1950, more than half the wheels of railroad propulsion would be turned by the internal combustion engine. Steam locomotives worked out their serviceable lives on such roads as the Missouri-Kansas-Texas; the Lehigh Valley; the Wabash; the Gulf, Mobile, and Ohio; the Frisco; and the Missouri Pacific. In 1953, the Southern Railway System became the country's largest all-diesel line. Others, like the Illinois Central; the Union Pacific; the Nickel Plate Road; and the Duluth, Missabe, and Iron Range were not so hasty in sending their steamers to scrap.

At mid-decade, however, it was apparent that the days of using fire to heat water as a method of moving the trains were quickly coming to a close. Even the Chesapeake and Ohio, which had a loyalty to on-line coal traffic, had only a few of the super-power engines built by the Lima Locomotive Works left on its roster.

But one railway held to steam longer than the rest. Spanning the Virginias and reaching into Ohio, the coal-carrying Norfolk and Western had developed steam power to such an extent that its engines were comparable to—and in many instances better than—the products of the Electro-Motive Division of General Motors and other manufacturers exploiting Rudolf Diesel's invention.

Building locomotives of its own design at the company's vast Roanoke, Virginia, shops, the N&W developed what it called the "Modern Coal-Burning Steam Locomotive (i.e., a unit with a high capacity boiler, roller bearings on all engine and tender wheels, one-piece cast-steel frame, improved counterbalancing, and complete mechanical and pressure lubrication)." Culminating in three classes—the "A," "J," and "Y6"—these "Finest Steam Engines Ever Built" gave the road a versatile trio that could handle efficiently virtually any assignment for which they were called upon. The A, with its 2-6-6-4 wheel configuration, could easily move long coal and time-freight trains over the flatter portions of the N&W or pinch-hit on passenger trains at better than seventy miles per hour. The J was a 4-8-4 high-speed streamlined passenger

Amid the staybolts and steam gauges of a locomotive cab, Bernard Cliff feeds the white-hot firebox of 4-8-0 M2 engine 1148.

engine capable of clipping off 15,000 miles a month at up to a 110 miles per hour, while the Y6 was the workhorse of the railroad, a 2-8-8-2 packing a heavy punch for the mountain grades and curvature of the coalfield branch lines.

Together, these three types accounted for eighty-four percent of the railway's passenger miles and more than ninety percent of freight-ton miles though they comprised little more than a third of the locomotives rostered. The N&W accomplished this by "dieselizing" in theory, with modern maintenance and modern servicing installations and principles both in the shop and out on the road, resulting in a higher availability and less time in getting over the line.

Stemming from a fierce faith in the bituminous coal business that was the biggest part of its revenue, the N&W was constantly tinkering with ways to improve on its stable of steam engines, whether by modernizing K2 Mountains to resemble the racy Js or by building forty-five new S1a 0-8-0 switchers, the last steam locomotives assembled in the United States. In 1955 the Norfolk and Western was the last Class I railroad in the country that had yet to employ a single diesel unit.

But it was clear that rising labor costs and an increasingly arduous, as well as expensive, effort in locating component parts would soon end the fabled era of steam. It would be only a matter of time before the N&W, failing with its last coal-burning locomotive, a steam-turbine-electric model called the "Jawn Henry," would have to make the reluctant decision to dieselize. Only a handful of stubby short lines and dinky

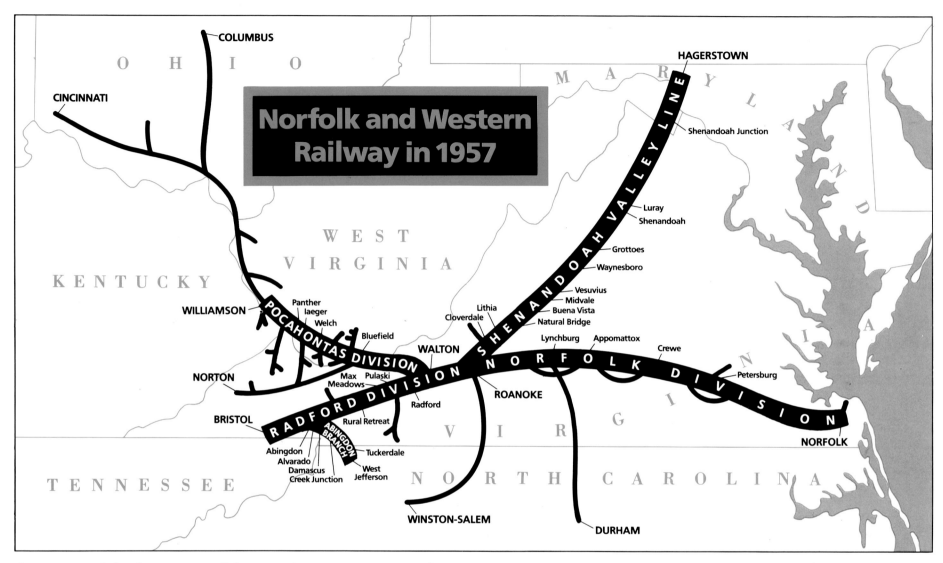

Norfolk and Western Railway in 1957

OHIO

COLUMBUS

CINCINNATI

WEST VIRGINIA

KENTUCKY

WILLIAMSON

Panther
Iaeger
Welch

NORTON

POCAHONTAS DIVISION

Bluefield

Max Pulaski
Meadows

Radford

RADFORD DIVISION

BRISTOL

Rural Retreat

ABINGDON BRANCH

Abingdon
Alvarado
Damascus
Creek Junction

Tuckerdale

West
Jefferson

TENNESSEE

WINSTON-SALEM

MARYLAND

HAGERSTOWN

Shenandoah Junction

Luray
Shenandoah

Grottoes

Waynesboro

Vesuvius
Midvale
Buena Vista
Natural Bridge

Lithia
Cloverdale

SHENANDOAH VALLEY LINE

WALTON

Lynchburg   Appomattox

Crewe

NORFOLK DIVISION

Petersburg

ROANOKE

VIRGINIA

NORFOLK

NORTH CAROLINA

DURHAM

factory switchers would remain to carry on the American steam locomotive's proud history.

Winston Link was deeply aware of this impending loss as he drove his 1952 Buick convertible eastward in the early darkness, negotiating rolling Route 250 toward Waynesboro. From his copy of the N&W timetable, he knew that he would see at least a northbound passenger train go through on the line that extended up the Shenandoah Valley from Roanoke to Hagerstown, Maryland.

In Waynesboro he located the depot and found it to be an unusual two-level frame affair in which the N&W tracks crossed under and perpendicular to the main line of the rival Chesapeake and Ohio. Though the more lordly accommodations of the C&O's *Fast Flying Virginian* and *George Washington* were to be encountered upstairs, they did not interest Link as much as the N&W's steam-drawn train.

Inside the depot Link found an amiable telegrapher with whom he soon struck up a conversation. Ascertaining that it would be "a while" before the arrival of the expected passenger train, the visitor was invited to "make himself at home and have a look around."

At Waynesboro, a layover and turn-around point for local freights from Roanoke and Shenandoah, the Norfolk and Western had a small wayside yard to handle interchange with the C&O in addition to a skeleton car-repair shop and locomotive-refueling facilities. It was not unusual to find N&W locomotives straddling the turntable or a yard engine, used to shift freight for the town's industries, simmering on the service track.

Inspecting the premises, Link became aware of the traditional appurtenances of railroading that he knew had not endured elsewhere: a Seth Thomas clock on the wall...the sweet scent of kerosene...men in bib overalls, bright bandannas, and Kromer caps...the chatter of telegraphic communications...warmth from a pot-bellied stove...the ruby glow of a lantern.

As he waited, 2nd 95, a southbound time freight with merchandise from New York and New England, stopped and shifted out a set-off, its giant, home-built Y6 2-8-8-2 lumbering with a big-shouldered swagger, then rumbling as it pumped air into its charge before storming off. Looming out of the darkness at the end of the departing train's toe-tapping, dancing cars, a ghostly figure swung from the rear of the caboose, made a dead-eye swipe at an order fork, and was swallowed up by the night.

Then, precisely at the appointed 9:23 P.M. arrival time, Train Two dashed into the station and squealed to a stop at the brick platform. There was a clatter of baggage carts, and the able-looking engineer dropped down from the deckplate with a long-necked oiler while the panting K2a locomotive strove to catch its breath. This symphony in steam was overseen by a ramrod-straight conductor, who, in between cordially assisting his passengers to board and disembark, kept impatiently eyeing the open-faced dial of a gold-cased pocket watch. Just as quickly as it came, the short express with through cars for New York, including a Pullman, was gone in a veil of smoke and steam, its passage marked only by a pair of receding red markers and the bouncing blink of the yellow position-light signal moving from vertical to horizontal display.

Link was addicted! What he experienced that night and had known since boyhood had to be committed to photographic paper before the historic rituals of railroading disappeared forever. As little as he had seen at Waynesboro, how much was there that could be captured at other locations on the Norfolk and Western? He realized that the possibilities were tremendous. And he believed he could do the job best by shooting mostly at night, when he could control the lighting. Besides, darkness seemed symbolic of the glamour and romance associated with railroading. His would be a steady diet of steam and steel beneath the stars.

The next day, as Link was shooting a series of pictures to promote the sale of air conditioners, the hot, steamy exhaust plumes of locomotives kept rushing down the track of his mind. That evening—January 21, 1955—he returned to the Waynesboro station with his 4 x 5 Graphic camera and parallel-system, synchronized-flash equipment and, with the help of a friend he had enlisted, made several exposures of the trains and depot. Later, when he developed and printed these images in his East 34th Street studio in New York, Link's spirits soared; he realized that the results were every bit as good as he had calculated and anticipated.

Thus encouraged, he fired off a letter to the N&W's Public Relations and Advertising Department asking for assistance with the monumental endeavor he was now planning, and for background information on the railway.

"Have you ever noticed the dearth of photographs of railroad scenes at night?" he wrote. "I would like to make a series of well-planned night photographs of exceptional quality and interest showing the railroad at work as the passenger sleeps. For human interest, I would like to show an employee in every picture.

"On this proposed long-range project, all I could hope for from your railroad would be some sort of cooperation in picking locations and obtaining necessary permission to enter yards," he continued. "Do you think your management would be favorable?"

Satisfied that he had adequately stated his case, Link enclosed a print of his first railroad night shot, Train Two pulling into Waynesboro, along with two proof sheets of his outstanding advertising work. All he could do now was to anxiously await the N&W's reply.

Right: Steam locomotives have fascinated both young and old throughout time. Here, spellbound boys pay homage to steam's magic as Train Two slips to a stop at Waynesboro. A similar scene in January 1955 inspired O. Winston Link to initiate his project.

Above: Car Inspector J. N. Kite shines his lantern beside the cheery warmth of a pot-bellied stove before having to wrestle with the cold, stiff journal lids out in the Waynesboro Yard.

Right: Transforming the placid brick platform into a cavalcade of commotion, "The New York Train" impatiently pauses at Waynesboro on its nightly sojourn up the Shenandoah Valley. Conductor L. M. Richardson checks his schedule, while the Hangar brothers handle mail and express packages.

Overleaf, left: Engineer Howard Ruble anoints the arthritic appendages of Class K2a No. 130 on a rainy, rust-begetting night.

Overleaf, right: Waynesboro station Telegrapher Troy Humphries checks train orders with the Shenandoah Division dispatcher in

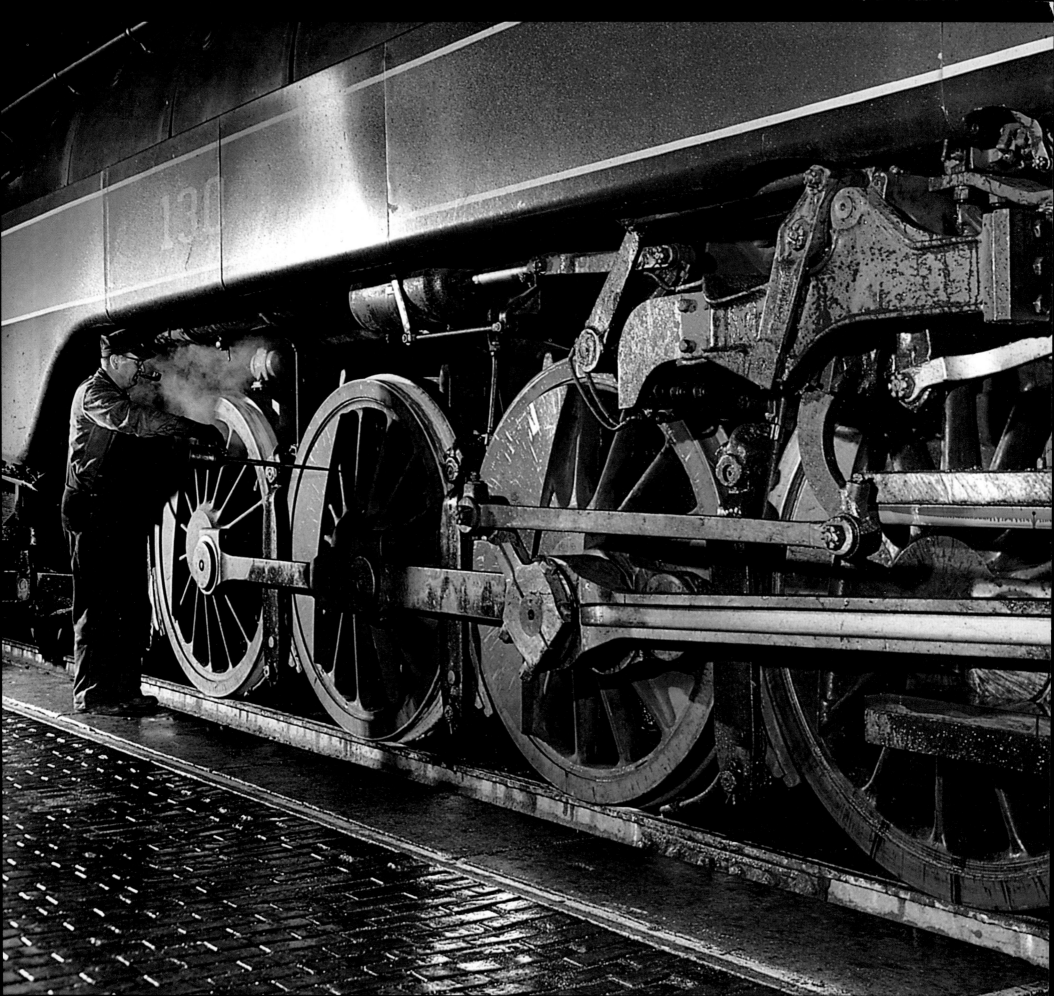

Charging toward Roanoke, 2-8-8-2 No. 2142 ducks under the main
line of the Chesapeake and Ohio.

Above: Poised to receive train orders on the fly, Conductor F. Y. Knight of Shenandoah takes aim from a caboose platform. The intent veteran's fingers will split the fork, snapping the taut string as he snares the "flimsies" around his upper arm.
Right: The tempo of a Seth Thomas clock paces work in the Waynesboro station. Troy Humphries sits at the telegraph table, while Bernie Cliff masquerades as a conductor examining waybills.

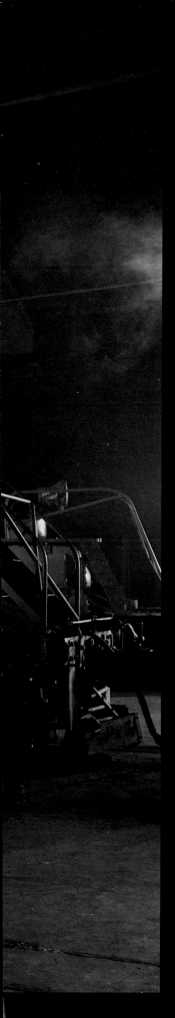

Passing through the Shenandoah Valley on the southbound N&W Train One, O. Winston Link reread the letter he had received from Ben Bane Dulaney of the railroad's Public Relations and Advertising Department.

"Your photo of Train Two at Waynesboro is excellent," Dulaney had written. "However, it is not one that we would ordinarily approve for publication, because at the time the picture was taken, the locomotive pop valve was lifted (denoting a poor firing practice from feeding an excessive amount of fuel to the firebox, something not prescribed by the ever-efficient champion of the coal-burning locomotive).

2

This Railroad Is a Living Thing

"But do not think we are criticizing your splendid picture," the publicist continued. "We shall be happy to grant you permission to take photographs on our properties. If you will advise us when you want to be on the railroad, we shall be glad to cooperate by picking suitable photo locations for you. We appreciate your interest in the Norfolk and Western and look forward to working with you."

Left: The 40-stall Shaffers Crossing Roundhouse at Roanoke was the pride of the N&W. In the heyday of steam the Shaffers Crossing Locomotive Department could clean the fire of, inspect, coal, sand, water, and turn 135 engines every 24 hours.

The next time he was on assignment in Staunton, Link worked in a trip to Roanoke and boarded the train at Waynesboro on a chilly March morning. He reflected on the contrast in lifestyles as he watched the unfurling countryside. He had come from nerve-jangling Manhattan streets to the misty Blue Ridge Mountains. Pausing briefly at such stops as Buena Vista, Troutville, and Cloverdale, whose names reflect the beauty surrounding them, the tuscan-colored train blasted onward toward the "Star City of the South." Arriving at the modernistic Roanoke passenger station, Link was amazed at the beehive of railroading activity. There were steam locomotives everywhere!

From out of the east, Time Freight No. 85 flashed by with a Class A 2-6-6-4 on the point. An S1a 0-8-0 sped through hauling the Pullman *McDowell County.* An A and a Y6 teamed up in toting a long coal extra toward the Tidewater piers at Lambert's Point. A powerful J-class 4-8-4 sighed softly on the east end of Track Three, ready to receive a hand-off in the form of the *Pocahontas.* This was Roanoke, headquarters and hub of the Norfolk and Western, where five main-line routes radiate north, south, east, west, and southwest.

Nestled in a natural bowl beneath majestic Mill Mountain, the downtown depot is flanked by the massive system shops to the east, the general office buildings and Shaffers Crossing Terminal to the west. Across the street from the station, a knoll is crowned by the company's showcase, the Hotel Roanoke, an elegant English Tudor-style inn.

Link was intrigued by the photographic possibilities of the waiting room, ticket office, and train board as well as the aluminum, glass, terrazzo, and tile decor designed by Raymond Loewy and Associates in a 1949 remodeling. In the upstairs concourse, an old-time train caller announced the departure of yet another connection in a pronounced Virginia drawl: "Traaiin Numbuh Eee'levuunn is nooww ready for boarding on traack fooah…Rocky Mount, Bassett, Martinsville, Mayodan, Walnut Cove 'n Winston-Salem. Allll aaaboaard for Nawth Carliinah 'n points south!"

Through the well-manicured grounds of the Hotel Roanoke, Link made his way to the corporate headquarters on North Jefferson Street, where he located the Public Relations offices. He was ushered in immediately and almost as quickly became fast friends with the disarming, chain-smoking Ben Bane Dulaney. Dulaney, who would act as a liaison between Link and the N&W, was born and brought up in Washington, D.C., but his role with the railroad was cast as a child in Glade Spring, Virginia, where he summered with his maternal grandparents. Fascinated by the trains, he was a constant visitor to the small town station (where an uncle was a telegrapher) from the time he arrived on No. 41, then referred to as the *New York, Chattanooga, & New Orleans Limited* (later named the *Pelican,* in honor of Louisiana's state bird). He occupied himself doing odd jobs and bumming rides on the Salt Branch shifter.

Educated at The University, as Virginia graduates like to say, Dulaney served as a *Wash-*

ington Post editor and *Time* correspondent before he combined his two loves—writing and railroading—by joining the N&W organization as Manager of News and Community Services. Avidly interested in the railroad's history and an authority on its background and personality, he commenced to lecture an attentive Link.

The formation of the Norfolk and Western was sixty years in the making. Steel rails were laid through a maze of bankruptcies and bureaucratic confoundments, through civil war, epidemics, and engineering nightmares. The story began in the early 1830s when the budding town of Petersburg, Virginia, needed a means to move its goods to shipping on the nearby James River. Already the northern terminus of the second railroad in the South, the aggressive little trading center, barely emerging from Colonial times, had only a hopelessly rutted road to the City Point docks and the commerce of Northern markets. Petitioning the Virginia General Assembly, the incipient railroad's promoters pleaded that when, as was often the case, the pike became an impassable quagmire in the rain and snow, it took nearly as long to make the eight-mile trip to the James River wharf as did the rest of the voyage by ship to New York.

After a three-year debate, permission to build the line was granted, and the City Point Rail Road was incorporated on January 26, 1836. More than two years later—on September 7, 1838—the first train pulled by the little locomotive *Powhatan* (built by William Norris of Philadelphia, who also built a sister engine named *Pocahontas* a year later) struggled from Petersburg to City Point on thin straps of imported English rail laid on wooden stringers over stone crossties. This was the humble beginning of the Norfolk and Western.

Meanwhile, railroad fever had infected Lynchburg, located at the base of the Blue Ridge and served by the James River and Kanawha Canal. City fathers envisioned a rail link over the mountains to the New River, which would open up the Midwest. It was to be nineteen years, however, before a spade was to be turned on Lynchburg's railroad.

The New River had been declared unfit for navigation, save anything smaller than a rowboat, and Lynchburg's leaders began dreaming of an overland rail route, perhaps even to the Mississippi. After two name changes, the Virginia and Tennessee was chartered, and in 1850 the first rails were aimed at the Peaks of Otter and the blue mountains beyond. After six years of struggle to surmount two chains of mountains (the Blue Ridge and Allegheny ranges), the rails threaded through southwest Virginia and touched Bristol on the Tennessee line.

Two more railroads were under construction in the Old Dominion during this period. Both had to solve engineering problems that were considered unsolvable in that day.

Chartered in 1846, the Southside Railroad between Petersburg and Lynchburg was proposed to compete with the prosperous James River canal interests. The water people fought the line bitterly before the Commonwealth gave its blessing, but a greater problem was presented by the yawning chasm of the Appomattox River near Farmville. The solution was a 3,400-foot-long structure called High Bridge, a true marvel of its time consisting of twenty piers made from 3,766,000 bricks. Completion of the span in 1853 allowed the line to open a year later and "up trains" and "down trains" were scheduled between the termini, stopping along the way at such proprietary pastures as Sutherland's, Ford's, Wilson's, and Rice's, as well as Blacks & Whites (now Blackstone), where a population of two colors of sheep prevailed.

East of Petersburg, the old seaport of Norfolk longed to have an inland rail link. An apparently bottomless bog known as the Great Dismal Swamp was keeping commerce away from its all-weather harbor. The Norfolk and Petersburg was authorized in 1851 but had no luck in dealing with the depth of the swamp until it hired a twenty-seven-year-old civil engineer by the name of William Mahone in 1853.

Under Mahone's direction, workers cleared a wide right-of-way, dug drainage ditches, and laid a corduroy mat of trees, roots, and fill for the rails to rest upon. And the road was planned wide enough so that it could be double-tracked later, a foresight thought foolish in that early day. Having conquered the swamp, in spite of enduring acute labor shortages and an epidemic of yellow fever, Mahone set his sights on Suffolk and then laid fifty-two miles of perfectly straight railroad to Petersburg in what is still one

of the longest tangents in the country. The last spike was driven in 1858.

Now there was a rail route from Tidewater to Tennessee. The three lines—the Norfolk and Petersburg, the Southside (which had absorbed the Appomattox Railroad, successor to the City Point Rail Road, in 1854), and the Virginia and Tennessee—fed each other traffic and prospered. By 1860, connecting roads at Petersburg and Lynchburg to the north and from Bristol to the south allowed a direct rail route, utilizing the three Virginia roads, from New York and Norfolk to New Orleans and Memphis.

The new-found affluence of this system was not to last long, however, as the "War Between the States" all but wrecked the three railroads. Repeated Northern raids damaged both the Southside and the V&T, and the Norfolk and Petersburg was torn up by Rebel forces in retreat. At the end of the struggle, things were in a pitiful state, with the Southside being the richest of the three roads, having a balance of $675,000 in its treasury—all but $3,592 of the sum in worthless Confederate currency.

It took the resourceful William Mahone, the man who built the Norfolk and Petersburg, to put the twisted tracks back together. Now a famous Southern general and hero of the "Battle of the Crater," Mahone, already president of the N&P, gained the presidency of the Southside in 1865 and called upon workers to rebuild the two roads with only a wage of "meat, bread, and a promise to pay."

Two years later, in 1867, advocating a railroad consolidation program, Mahone was elected president of the Virginia and Tennessee. Amidst cries of monopoly, Mahone won a three-year fight to convince Virginia's legislators that the three roads over which he presided should naturally be combined, wooing the politicians with elaborate dinner parties featuring terrapin soup and champagne. Victorious, he merged the three roads into the Atlantic, Mississippi, and Ohio Railroad in November 1870, uniting the

After making a "watch comparison" in the call office at Bluefield, Fireman Russell F. Bussey poses for Link prior to starting on a run back to his home terminal at Roanoke.

408 miles of road from Norfolk to Bristol under one company.

Mahone rebuilt the newly formed AM&O with English capital, renewing the worn-out rails and replacing the rolling stock with better locomotives and cars. A stickler for every detail, he constantly roamed from one end of the line to the other on inspection trips in a party of two handcars, one for himself, the other for his baggage and servant. In spite of this fastidiousness—he even designed and built the station houses—Mahone could not stave off the Panic of 1873 and the resulting economic depression, and by 1876 the line was in receivership.

The AM&O was purchased at public auction in 1881 for $8,605,000 by Clarence H. Clark and Associates, Philadelphia financiers who reorganized the property as the Norfolk and Western Railroad.

Prior to the 1880s, the newly organized Norfolk and Western and its predecessors had depended upon the products of an agrarian South—cotton, lumber, tobacco, grains, and cattle—for the majority of its revenue. But a civil engineer representing the Clark interests named Frederick J. Kimball dug a pen knife into an outcropping of coal at a place called Abbs Valley in Virginia's far southwest corner and changed all that.

President of the Shenandoah Valley Railroad, another Clark property that had been half-heartedly building southward from Hagerstown, Maryland, Kimball had long been intrigued by reports of an unbelievable thir- 27 teen-foot bank of "black diamonds" in Tazewell County. Studying a stack of surveys, some dating all the way back to the time of Thomas Jefferson, he decided to see for himself the spectacular seam. By buggy and by horseback he found the place in the wilderness and took samples of the magic mineral that the village blacksmith used to fire his forge. The coal's qualities proved to be far superior to anything yet found, and Kimball immediately set about the problem of transporting it by rail.

Kimball first connected the Shenandoah Valley to a junction with the N&W at a place called Big Lick in 1882, induced by a cash offering by the town's four hundred inhabitants. A car hoist was erected to change out trucks, compensating for the difference in gauges of the sister companies' tracks.

Its name changed to Roanoke, the hamlet began growing from that moment, and a year later the town's first industry, the Roanoke Machine Works—billed as the "greatest car and locomotive manufacturing plant in the South"—was established to service the equipment of the SV and N&W. The enterprise employed some twelve hundred men, mostly rowdy Irishmen kept in check by Father J. W. Lynch, who held Mass in a passenger coach until Saint Andrew's Catholic Church was built. In 1883, the general offices of the two railroads were moved from Hagerstown and Lynchburg to the vibrant little city of Roanoke, further stimulating that city's growth. (By the 1950s the N&W would come to employ more than six thousand of Roanoke's citizens.)

Frederick Kimball, meanwhile, being a vice-president of the N&W also, persuaded that road's board of directors to build a branch line called the New River Extension from Radford to tap the rich vein of bituminous at Abbs Valley. The first car of coal was loaded on March 12, 1883. Though the mine—Pocahontas Number One—produced only 54,542 tons of coal that first year, the destiny of the railroad was decided when the first lump left the chute, singing a song of spilling coffers. ("Carrier of Fuel Satisfaction," the N&W would come to call itself in reference to the 130 varieties of coals found in the territory served by its trains.) By 1957 it would be hauling over sixty million tons of coal—more than ten percent of the total production in the United States.

As a reward for his insight, Kimball was elevated to the presidency of the N&W in 1883, and he became the guiding force in the line's growth for the next twenty years. While the mine at Pocahontas (the new name for Abbs Valley, in honor of the colliery and the Indian princess of Captain John Smith fame) flourished, Kimball, knowing that he had only scratched the surface in cashing in on vast coal deposits, dreamed of a route to the Ohio River to open up the beds of coal that lay along West Virginia's border with Kentucky and Virginia. Others who controlled the railroad's capital dallied through the remainder of the decade, preoccupied with a line that never materialized to Washington, D.C., or with worthless iron ore deposits along a never-finished line intended to connect with the Atlantic and Yadkin near the North Carolina line.

In February 1890 an opportunity arose to buy the Scioto Valley and New England, a 121-mile pike extending from Coal Grove, Ohio, west along the Ohio River to Portsmouth, then up to Columbus. Kimball seized upon the option, snapping up the road for $3,000,000 in preferred stock. A month later, contracts were let for the construction of the Ohio Extension, the most ambitious project the N&W would ever undertake.

Starting simultaneously from Elkhorn, the end of one of a series of coal branches that had been constructed off the New River Extension from Bluefield, and from Kenova on the Ohio River, fifteen contractors, five thousand men, and a multitude of mules, oxen, and horses slowly wound their way toward each other through the wilds of West Virginia. Work was also under way on a five-span, 3,886-foot bridge and approach viaduct at Kenova that would connect with the SV&NE at Sheridan after crossing the wide Ohio into the Buckeye State.

Considerable difficulty was experienced in the 191-mile route, as "treacherous material" was encountered in the drilling of eight tunnels during the harsh Appalachian winters. At long last, the two halves met and were joined at four P.M. on September 22, 1892, near Hatfield, West Virginia, almost within sight of the ancestral homeplace of Devil Anse Hatfield, patriarch of the famous clan that feuded with the McCoys, their neighbors on the Kentucky side of the Tug River. (In fact, several members of the Hatfield family held timber contracts to supply crossties for the N&W's roadbed.)

With the opening of the Ohio Extension, the railroad now had a main line stretching nearly seven hundred miles from Norfolk to connections at Columbus with the markets of the Midwest. Satisfied with his efforts, Kimball turned his energies toward developing coal traffic, particularly to the industrial perimeter of the Great Lakes. Today, more than seventy spurs protrude like the branches of a plum tree to pluck the production of the Tug River, Clinch Valley, Buchanan, Pocahontas, Thacker, and Kenova coalfields. It has been said that the Norfolk and Western could abandon every mile of its track except that between Bluefield and Kenova and still turn a profit.

Notable expansion continued under Kimball through the 1890s as the Shenandoah Valley was merged outright in 1890 and the Clinch Valley District was finished to a Louisville and Nashville connection from Bluefield to Norton in 1891. Then all this sudden growth, combined with the Panic of 1893 and its subsequent downturn in business, sapped the Norfolk and Western Railroad. It went bankrupt and was then reorganized as the Norfolk and Western Railway on September 24, 1896. Recovering quickly, it absorbed the Roanoke and Southern Railway between Roanoke and Winston-Salem, North Carolina, and the Lynchburg and Durham, between those two points, the same year. In 1897, the Roanoke Machine Works came into the fold as Roanoke Shops.

Finally, the physical framework of the Norfolk and Western as O. Winston Link would come to know it was finished when the Cincinnati, Portsmouth and Virginia, a hundred-mile line between the two Ohio cities, was purchased in 1901. Two years later, Frederick J. Kimball, who is rightly considered the "father" of the railroad even though it had been born more than sixty years before he appeared on the scene, passed away.

With its network of track completed, the N&W continued to grow, investing millions of dollars and eventually organizing into five operating entities (the Norfolk, Shenandoah, Radford, Pocahontas, and Scioto divisions). In the first ten years after World War II alone, over $216,000,000 was spent for capital improvements, ranging from painting the station at Peebles, Ohio, out on the "Peavine" (as the Cincinnati District of the Scioto Division is nicknamed) to boring 7,052 feet through Elkhorn Mountain in West Virginia to create what was then (1949) the longest double-track tunnel in the world. A pacesetter in the rail industry, the N&W could also boast of installing the first fully automatic switching operation—at Portsmouth Terminal in 1955—and of owning sixty thousand freight cars, more cars per mile than any American railroad longer than 250 miles, among other accomplishments.

Preparedness over the years resulted in an ability to carry anything movable, anywhere, anytime, for anybody. There was nothing too big or too delicate for the Norfolk and Western; it could move a 430,000-pound generator from Hagerstown to Bristol or three Roanoke polio victims in iron lungs to Richmond.

Hauling coal and freight was the N&W's main job, but it also provided a widely admired passenger service, with clean coaches, sparkling diners, and posh lounge cars traversing what one railroad editor termed "a vast passenger wasteland." Introducing the *Pocahontas* in 1926 and the *Cavalier* a year later for the Norfolk to Cincinnati-Columbus trade, the N&W also operated three trains in conjunction with the Southern Railway—the *Birmingham Special*, the *Pelican*, and the silvery *Tennessean* between Lynchburg and Bristol on a New York–Washington and Deep South route. In addition, there were Nos. One and Two up the Shenandoah Valley and the *Cannon Ball* between Norfolk and Richmond, forwarded from Petersburg by the Atlantic Coast Line. And there were numerous locals featuring air-conditioned coaches to such secondary main-line terminals as Durham, Norton, and Winston-Salem, as well as accommodations of some sort (often meaning mixed trains) to nearly every branch line point.

Finest of the N&W's passenger fleet by a long shot, flung from the bow of a famous Indian chief, was the crack *Powhatan Arrow*, a sleek all-coach streamliner on a sixteen-hour schedule between Norfolk and Cincinnati. Introduced in 1946, Trains 25 and 26 were updated three years later with custom-built equipment from Pullman-Standard featuring a "boat tail" tavern-lounge-observation car to round out the rear of the usual three coaches and a diner.

Recognized by many as "America's Finest Train," rivaling the *Daylights* of the Southern Pacific and the *Twentieth Century Limited* of the New York Central, the *"Powtan"* certainly painted a picture of beauty as it raced along the broad Ohio River bottom lands on a fall day, rustling the sun-scorched sheaths of corn. Why, the N&W reasoned, just because Welch, West Virginia, didn't have the population of a Cleveland or a Chicago was no reason its citizens should have to depart in less luxury when it came time to take a trip!

Electrician's Helper J. W. Dalhouse stares "eye-to-eye" at a K2a 127 engine as he affectionately polishes its headlight in the Shaffers Crossing Roundhouse.

Reflected in all the accomplishments of the N&W was the pride of those who worked the line, and no one in any vocation took more pride in his profession than the locomotive engineer. He was a celebrity in the community in which he lived. Like the red, five-pointed designs on the gauntlet gloves he wore, he was a "star" to those many who looked up to him, as much as any Hollywood actor.

For many young men dreaming of a life on the rails, the engineer was a hero to be emulated, and the railroad was always in need of men with eager minds and strong backs. Road Foreman of Engines L. H. Blankenship (railroaders usually went by their initials) wanted a job on the locomotives so badly as a youth that he arose at five o'clock every morning and stoked the boilers of a Narrows, Virginia, tannery, his only pay the thrill of blowing the worktime whistle!

In the days before locomotives were "pooled," lending to a standard appearance, enginemen would spend their off-days polishing their personalized "possessions," burnishing boilers with signal oil or affixing brass eagles or Masonic emblems to headlights. The fact that the Norfolk and Western built its own locomotives (nearly every one on the line since 1927) added to this feeling of possessiveness. One N&W engineer, Thomas W. Goodwin of Roanoke, even took his affection for his locomotive to his grave, his last request being that a stonecutter carve a granite replica of his beloved little No. 227, a Class G 2-8-0, to rest atop his tombstone.

Pride was also manifested in a well-maintained roadbed and right-of-way. The main lines were laid on fifteen inches of limestone with rail weighing 131 pounds per yard—much heavier than the industry average. Coal is a heavy commodity and rail of anything less wouldn't wear on the curves.

More than five thousand maintenance-of-way workers labored upon the smooth steel carpet of the Norfolk and Western, utilizing the latest in mechanized equipment. Some section foremen even made the men in their gangs dress the ballast along the berm to the tune of a tautly stretched string. If this sounds eccentric, consider that the company awarded cash prizes in an Annual Track Inspection, an October tradition since 1887. The competition was judged on six items—line and surface, switches and frogs, ditches and roadbed, right-of-way, station grounds, and road crossings. In other manifestations of enthusiasm, many went so far as to cultivate shrubbery spelling out "N&W" at their section dwellings, and one depot had a flower box a block long!

Finally, just being "in the service," as working for the Norfolk and Western was called, was reward in itself. Most N&W employees never drew a paycheck from another company. Conductor G. S. Stanley put in more than a million miles on the passenger trains that plied the "Punkin' Vine" between Roanoke and Winston-Salem. W. P. Bugg put in sixty-two years, ten months, and sixteen days as a clerk at Norfolk Terminal.

Pensioners were treated to an annual bash by the railway, traveling by chartered trains and sleepers to outings at Virginia Beach, Lakeside Amusement Park in Salem, or Coney Island in Cincinnati. The proudest moment in the career of any N&W employee fortunate enough to have worked fifty years for the company came with the awarding in the president's office of the "Diamond Insignia" by the railway's Veterans Association.

The Norfolk and Western was an organization in which many worked their way up through the ranks. President R. H. Smith started as a chainman in a survey party during summer vacations from college, Chairman of the Board W. J. Jenks as a telegrapher, and General Manager C. H. Tabor a water boy. Each employee, whether a section man at Stone, Kentucky, a boilermaker at Bluefield, West Virginia, or an agent at Ashville, Ohio, was assured of having some say in the decision-making process through Better Service Clubs, which elected delegates to a yearly Better Service Conference.

It was not unusual to find families serving the N&W through several generations. The James family (grandfather William, son Edward, and grandson W. R.) had a continuous record in engine service from 1866—when General Mahone hired William as a fireman on the Norfolk and Petersburg—well into the 1950s. Entire households cast their lot with the N&W, including the six Spangler brothers of Peterstown, West Virginia, and the seven Cromer brothers of Roanoke. Another family, the Kegleys, held the jobs—conductor, engineer, fireman, and two brakemen—necessary to operate a freight train and, with the help of some cousins, they once actually did comprise an all-Kegley crew on the North Carolina Branch.

And families were started from relationships made through the Norfolk and Western. Case in point: Mr. and Mrs. T. A. Draper, the Clinch Valley couple who carried on a courtship by "sparking" over the wires during idle moments from their duties as telegraphers at the Richlands and Tom's Creek stations.

But the sense of "family" went beyond bloodlines. From one end of the railroad to the other, from the caller at Clare, Ohio, to the boys in the barney yard at the Lambert's Point piers, where the hoppers heaved their black burdens into the holds of hungry colliers, there were no two employees who didn't have some acquaintances in common. And their relationships were reinforced through the pages of the *Norfolk and Western Magazine,* founded in 1923, in a column called "The Folks Along the Line."

This feeling for the railroad resulted in a courtesy and friendliness that were N&W trademarks. Passenger Conductor R. Tucker Bowles of the Norfolk Division was known for wearing "a rose and a smile," and hardly an issue of the company magazine went by without a letter from some appreciative passenger commending the personable porter Willie Dillard. The railroad was inundated with protests when Engineer Alonzo Carter's run was changed, preempting his long-standing ritual of passing out bubble gum to youngsters as the *Powhatan Arrow* pulled into Lynchburg about the time local Sunday schools let out.

A good neighbor in the region it served, the railway promoted its six states (Maryland, Virginia, North Carolina, West Virginia, Kentucky, Ohio) as "The Land of Plenty," an area with a mighty potential for industry—and for living. In most of the counties along its route—thirty-seven in Virginia alone—the N&W was the largest taxpayer. It grew hand-in-hand with the communities it spawned. Roanoke had been a salt lick, Bluefield an azure-flowered meadow, and Williamson a patch of corn. There was no Crewe, no Ironton or Circleville to speak of before the N&W's rails arrived.

Realizing this partnership, the railway urged its employees to take part in local affairs and was quick to come to the aid of its communities in time of need. When Williamsburg, Ohio's, water supply ran perilously low in 1954, the N&W filled maintenance of way tenders and hauled nine thousand gallons of water a day to the town until the reserves were replenished. Conversely, it ran relief trains for refugees from Kenova and Portsmouth when the 1937 flood crippled the Ohio Valley. In the early morning hours of August 28, 1950, class M 4-8-0 locomotive No. 475 was dispatched on short notice to supply steam to the Clover Creamery Company of Roanoke, where a boiler had failed.

But to those who lived out along the line, in remote mountain cabins, rural southside Virginia or southwestern Ohio farms, and West Virginia coal camps, the N&W was more than just a railroad. It is in such country that trains are most a part of people's lives. Ever since the first teakettle engines caused cattle to bolt and dogs to bark, the passing of the trains has become as much a part of day-to-day life as the crowing of the cock or saying grace. ("I hear Number Four blowing for Belspring crossing, kids. Better finish breakfast and get off to school!")

Whether it be a wave from a friendly engineer or two flicks of a porch light answered by a playful whistle in the night, there is an unspoken communication between train crews and country folk. One elderly widow, Mrs. H. C. Chrisman, who for sixty years witnessed through her kitchen window the never-ceasing parade of panting locomotives as they climbed Christiansburg Mountain, summed it up when she said: "I am never lonely, not with all the people and trains that pass by my front door day and night."

People who live close to the railroad's right-of-way look out for the welfare of the trains, keeping a keen eye for hot boxes, shifting loads, or dragging equipment. A signal to the crew on the caboose indicates the nature of the problem; for instance, rubbing hands together means a stuck brake, holding the nose a hot box. In appreciation of these vigils, the train crews look after those living along the tracks. For Mr. and Mrs. William Lambert of Oakvale, West Virginia, it was Engineer R. H. Thompson stopping the second section of No. 16 on the morning of December 12, 1958, and running to roust them from their flaming house as Fireman J. W. Conner awakened them with the Class J locomotive's whistle. The crews would also leave lineside phone boxes unlocked so that the inhabitants of isolated areas would have some

means of communication in cases of emergency.

Not large as railroads go (there were twenty-seven in this country that had more miles of track), the N&W was, nonetheless, the story of United States railroading in microcosm, so much so that the Association of American Railroads often used the line as a subject for publicity shots and advertising campaigns. It was (and still is, after the Norfolk Southern merger) also an efficient money-making machine. Under Pennsylvania Railroad parentage until 1964, the N&W boasted one of the lowest operating ratios and the highest gross ton-mile per freight train averages in the business—and did it with steam. It has paid a handsome dividend to the stockholders in every year since 1901.

Having thus outlined the railroad's history, along with some of its spirit and ideals, Ben Dulaney took O. Winston Link to meet President R. H. Smith for final approval of his photography project. A gentleman of the old school who knew railroading from the inside-out, Smith was a man you didn't need an appointment to see.

Confidently, upon graduation in 1911 from Princeton, where he had been stroke on the first eight-oared varsity crew the university fielded, Baltimore-bred Robert Hall Smith III had remarked to the president of his class, "I'm going to be president of a railroad." Through his friend and classmate Arthur Maher, whose father N. D. Maher was general manager (and later president) of the Norfolk and Western, Smith first went to work for the company in

1910. Climbing the corporate ladder, he held the positions of masonry inspector, transitman, assistant roadmaster, and roadmaster in the Engineering Department before moving to the Operating Department as assistant superintendent of the Pocahontas Division. His rise continued to superintendent of the Radford Division, general superintendent of the Eastern General Division, general superintendent of the Western General Division, general manager, vice-president and general manager, vice-president of operations, and, in 1946, president.

Nicknamed "Race Horse" by his colleagues in reference to his gigantic stride, he was reputed to have walked every mile of track on his railroad. During World War II, he surprised a party of officials he had summoned to the Roanoke Passenger Station by setting out for Bluefield, 101 miles distant, on foot. Thinking they were going by plush private car, they were dressed to the nines, some even in white linen on the hot summer day. The purpose of their week-long journey, he informed them, was to pick up scrap as part of a metal drive promotion for the war effort, and to become as familiar with the roadbed as he was.

On another occasion, while waiting for a train at Atkins, Virginia, with Myron Decker, his personal secretary, Smith decided that time would permit them to walk to Marion, the next station, five miles distant. Smith, tall and rawboned and taking the ties two at a time, turned to his shorter secretary upon reaching their destination and declared emphatically: "Well, 'Deck,' that was a pretty good walk, wasn't it?" Winded and perspiring, Decker, who had been stumbling along the stones of the ballast, gasped: "Mister Smith, it might have been a good walk for you, but it was a hell of a long run for me!"

Smith didn't mince words when it came to carrying out the company's business and had a penchant for impromptu inspections and visits. One night, when he was a roadmaster on the Radford Division, he swooped down on some trackwalkers whose duties were to inspect several short tunnels in the vicinity of Shawsville, Virginia, for slides and falling rocks before the passing of each train. Catching them asleep, he confiscated their lanterns, which to their consternation were later presented as evidence at a hearing prior to their being disciplined.

Still, in spite of his sternness, R. H. Smith was known as a humanitarian. He liked to spend as much time as possible on the line, sleeping on the camp cars, taking meals with the men, and learning about their attitudes. He believed that "Politeness is the oil that lubricates the wheels of society. Good manners breed good feeling. A group of fellow workers whose contacts with each other are lubricated by good manners and good feeling will be a group which will turn out an attractive product."

For these reasons, he opted for a trackside office in the old General Office Building at the Roanoke system headquarters, rather than the eighth-floor penthouse in a newer structure next door. There, he could look out at the passing trains, and the engine crews would salute him as they moved by, leaning out of their locomotive cabs and doffing their hats in a grand, full-arm swing.

President Smith immediately appreciated Link's intentions and promised that word would be sent out to insure cooperation with the photographer all along the line. He had only two words of warning: Be careful and don't shoot engines spouting black smoke, because, as the slogan stenciled on the tender of every Norfolk and Western locomotive proclaimed, "Black Smoke is Waste."

During the next few months, Link rode the rear vestibules of passenger trains all over the far-reaching railroad that had grown to be 267 times as long as its City Point beginnings, plotting locations and taking notes for his dream to capture the nocturnal drama of steam railroading. Setting about his work with more enthusiasm than a newly inducted member of a volunteer fire brigade, O. Winston Link was now even more motivated than before he came to Roanoke. And he knew he'd better hurry, for already this last stronghold of steam power was about to receive its first diesels.

The Norfolk and Western that Link would come to know was much more than just an aggregate of 2,100 miles of track, tunnels, signals, shops, yards, and offices. It was also the brain and brawn of the railway's 21,000 loyal, conscientious employees, dedicated to making this the nation's best railroad—"Precision Transportation," they proudly called it.

Right: No railroad photographer worth his cinders could resist a study of a steam locomotive's driving wheels. Link proves he was no exception with this portrait of the running gear of Class E2a 4-6-2 No. 578 in the engine service building at Bluefield.

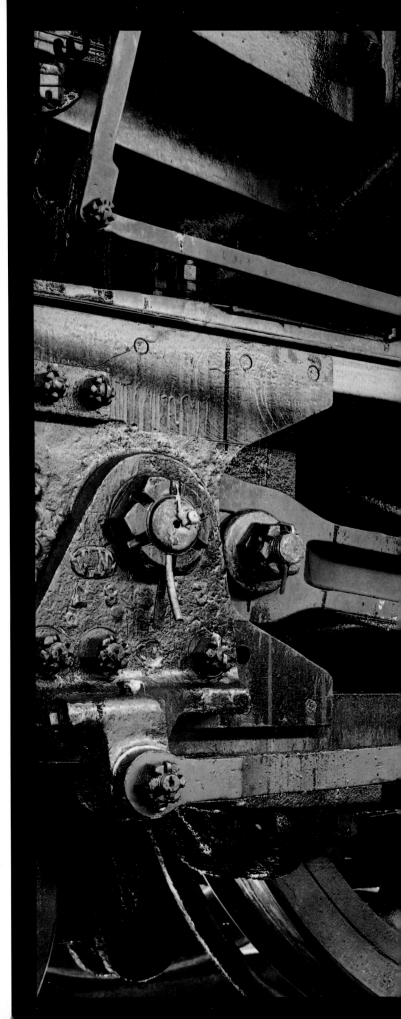

After making several trips to the N&W's facilities in the Roanoke area and a couple of pilgrimages westward along the main line to Bluefield, Winston Link began to concentrate photographically on the 238-mile Shenandoah Valley Line that extended southward from Hagerstown, Maryland, to Roanoke. Not only was this line closest to New York, but, more importantly, it was the first part of the railroad Link intended to document slated for dieselization.

The Shenandoah Valley Line dates back to 1870, the year it was incorporated in the three states— Maryland, West Virginia, and Virginia—through which it would pass. Chartered as the Shenandoah Valley Railroad, its purpose was to

3

Coal Smoke
down "The Valley"

open up a region rich in farmland and iron-ore deposits. Though it was not until May 1882 that the last of the 238 miles of track was laid, on June 18 of that year the first through train, a special, was operated over the entire line.

Initially the Shenandoah Valley Railroad flourished, but a depression hit the nation in 1884, and the line slipped into receivership the

Left: At Hagerstown Junction Operator Albert Blair holds an order fork high for the engineer of Train No. 1, just coming onto N&W rail for an early-morning romp to Roanoke over the Shenandoah Valley Line. From the cab of K2a 129, Fireman R. N. Good waves a greeting. 39

next year. After five years of failure the property was reorganized as the Shenandoah Valley Railway in September 1890.

Three months of a fresh start did little to stop the skid of the Shenandoah Valley Railway, and its track, 48 locomotives, 29 passenger cars, 961 freight cars, and many other assets were auctioned off on the Roanoke Court House steps on December 15, 1890. For the successful bid of $7,100,000, it was purchased by and merged outright on that date into the Norfolk and Western. Under the wing of the N&W the line, operated as its Maryland and Washington Division, eventually gained prosperity and became an important gateway for merchandise traffic moving between New England and other northern states and the South.

Ever since temporary facilities were moved from Sheperdstown, West Virginia, in 1881, the division point for the line has been maintained at a small (population 1,903, according to the 1950 census) but bustling railroad town named, appropriately enough, Shenandoah, Virginia. (Until 1889 the town was called Milnes, in honor of William Milnes, Jr., who founded the Shenandoah Iron Works there.) Here crews were changed, cars classified, locomotives serviced, and other shop work was performed.

In 1905 the segment between Roanoke and Hagerstown came to be known formally as the Shenandoah Valley Line. To the railroaders who worked on it, though, it was simply "The Valley."

In the early years of its operation the line enjoyed a healthy passenger business. Tourists flocked to see the scenic wonders of Natural Bridge, the Caverns of Luray, and to walk in hushed reverence on the Civil War battlefield of Antietam. With the increase in automobile travel, the Shenandoah Valley Line lost much of its importance for passengers in the 1920s, but it was still promoted with pride by the N&W. Until the Great Depression hit there were a pair of locals between Shenandoah and Hagerstown and two through trains each way, resplendent with Pullman sleepers and N&W dining and parlor cars between Roanoke and New York via a Pennsylvania Railroad connection.

The two sets of trains endured into the early 1950s, their ridership boosted seasonally by the many boarding schools, military academies, and colleges along the line. But by the time Link began to photograph the N&W the daylight runs (Trains 13 and 14) had been discontinued.

This left only the overnight Nos. 1 and 2 as the last passenger trains to ply the Shenandoah Valley Line. These trains were institutions to the inhabitants along their route, having served them for more than seventy years.

All passenger service on the line ended in February 1963, when diesel-drawn Trains 1 and 2, already shortened to a run between Roanoke and Waynesboro, were discontinued. But even today some of the older residents along the railroad recall the pleasure of sitting on the front porch after supper and listening to a steam powered "Number Two" charge up the valley, and how its booming chime whistle would carry after a soft summer rain.

Freight service on the line continued prosperously, however. These trains serviced such diverse industries as lumber finishers, rayon manufacturers, pharmaceutical plants, and limestone quarries. There was also heavy seasonal business during the apple and peach harvests and a steady, year-round flow from such trade as poultry and stock raising, tanning, and grain milling. On the south end of the line "Lone Star Shifters" made several daily movements out of Roanoke to a huge cement plant, located out on the Cloverdale Branch.

The Shenandoah Valley Line reached its high point in freight traffic during World War II. Shipments of coal and oil were often diverted to an all-rail route during the war because German submarines were striking ships moving north along the Atlantic coast. This brought an increase from a prewar average of 15,000 cars a month to an all-time peak of 53,952 in March of 1943. While the greatest gain was experienced in coal traffic, a total of twenty thousand carloads of oil alone moved over the line from January 1, 1943, to February 29, 1944. In freight-train movements, this translates to about thirty-six a day—each carrying over five thousand tons—up from a peace-time total of sixteen.

In order to physically handle the increase in traffic brought upon by the war, it was necessary to eliminate a "bottleneck" that developed between Vesuvius and Cold Spring. The congestion was caused by a combination of heavy gradient and single track, which prevented faster and opposing trains from passing the heavy coal drags moving northward over Lofton Hill. To ease the problem, it was decided in 1943 to double-track the ten-and-a-half miles between Vesuvius and Cold Spring. A wye track was also built at Lofton to permit the turning of helper engines.

The Shenandoah Valley Line, the northern part of the Shenandoah Division, more or less began at Hagerstown Junction. From this point the mileposts were numbered southward toward Roanoke. Here, an interchange with the Western Maryland and Pennsylvania railroads is protected by an interlocking plant called Hager Tower, the oldest of sixty plants maintained at one time or another by the N&W. It has been in continuing operation since 1863. South of the junction was Vardo Yard, an eleven-track classification facility with a roundhouse and a car-repair shop owned by the N&W but maintained and operated by the Pennsylvania Railroad.

South from Vardo the Shenandoah Valley Line threaded the broad Cumberland Valley until the tracks encountered the great trough of the Shenandoah Valley, south of the Potomac River below Sheperdstown. From Riverton, Virginia, to Vesuvius the tracks paralleled the south fork of the Shenandoah River for a distance of a hundred miles. From Glasgow to Buchanan they followed the historic James River. Below Buchanan the great valley narrowed down, and for most of the last twenty-five miles into Roanoke the railroad hugged curves around hillocks between channels cut by narrow creeks.

When Winston Link first undertook his N&W photography project he detoured all over the Shenandoah Valley Line and to other points along the railroad to scout intriguing photo locations. But early on he determined that he would concentrate on the more mountainous areas, where everything was in right up to the railroad, and on those lines that had the greatest traffic density, so that he could make the most of his time by having a greater number of train movements upon which to focus his cameras. Therefore work on the flatter portions of the railway, where the trains meandered through the backwoods, was pretty much ruled out. Also, there was no reason to wander way out to the western part of the railroad just to duplicate something he could take care of closer to home.

Another cause of Link's fascination with the Shenandoah Valley Line was the friendship he struck up with Walter Finney, a passenger engineer on the run from Roanoke to Shenandoah. Finney was one employee who did not worry too much about the consequences of violating N&W Operating Rule No. 587, which deemed that an engineman "must not permit an unauthorized person to ride on the engine"; Link knew that all he had to do to get permission from the crusty veteran was to climb up into his cab.

The N&W's Shenandoah Valley Line was a first-class piece of railroad, and the men who operated it were professionals in every way. Not even the blizzard that struck the Valley on March 7, 1932, leaving thirty-two inches of snow and wiping out all communications could stop these dedicated men from getting the trains through. In 1949 the division had the best safety record ever made on the whole N&W,

with only one injury in 2,225,000 man-hours worked, and by the time Link finished working along it, more than thirteen years—since January 1, 1944—had passed since the Shenandoah Valley Line saw a fatal injury.

But what impressed Link most about the line was the friendliness of the railroaders who worked upon it and of the people who lived along it. Everyone took an interest in Link's work and they all did their best to accommodate him and his helpers in every way. From Walter Finney's coffee, which warmed them on many cold nights spent out on the banks of Maury River, to the fried chicken they could count on in the Hester Fringer house at Lithia, the hospitality always flowed. The *Page News and Courier* did a story on his work there, impressed more by the fact that he was working without pay than by the immensity of his project, and even those persons who were paid for their services, such as Mrs. Zenobia, the proprietor of the Luray Motel, treated Link and his assistants like celebrities.

Of all the N&W routes on which he would focus his cameras, Link felt that he had accomplished his best work on "The Valley." It's a good thing he was satisfied, for time caught up with steam operation on the Shenandoah Valley Line on February 20, 1957, when K2a No. 129 pulled No. 1 into Roanoke with the last steam-powered train over the line. Link would be forced to look elsewhere on the Norfolk and Western in his impassioned quest to document and preserve the heritage of steam railroading.

Right: The name on the sign accurately captures the feeling of desolation at this lonely flagstop under the stars.

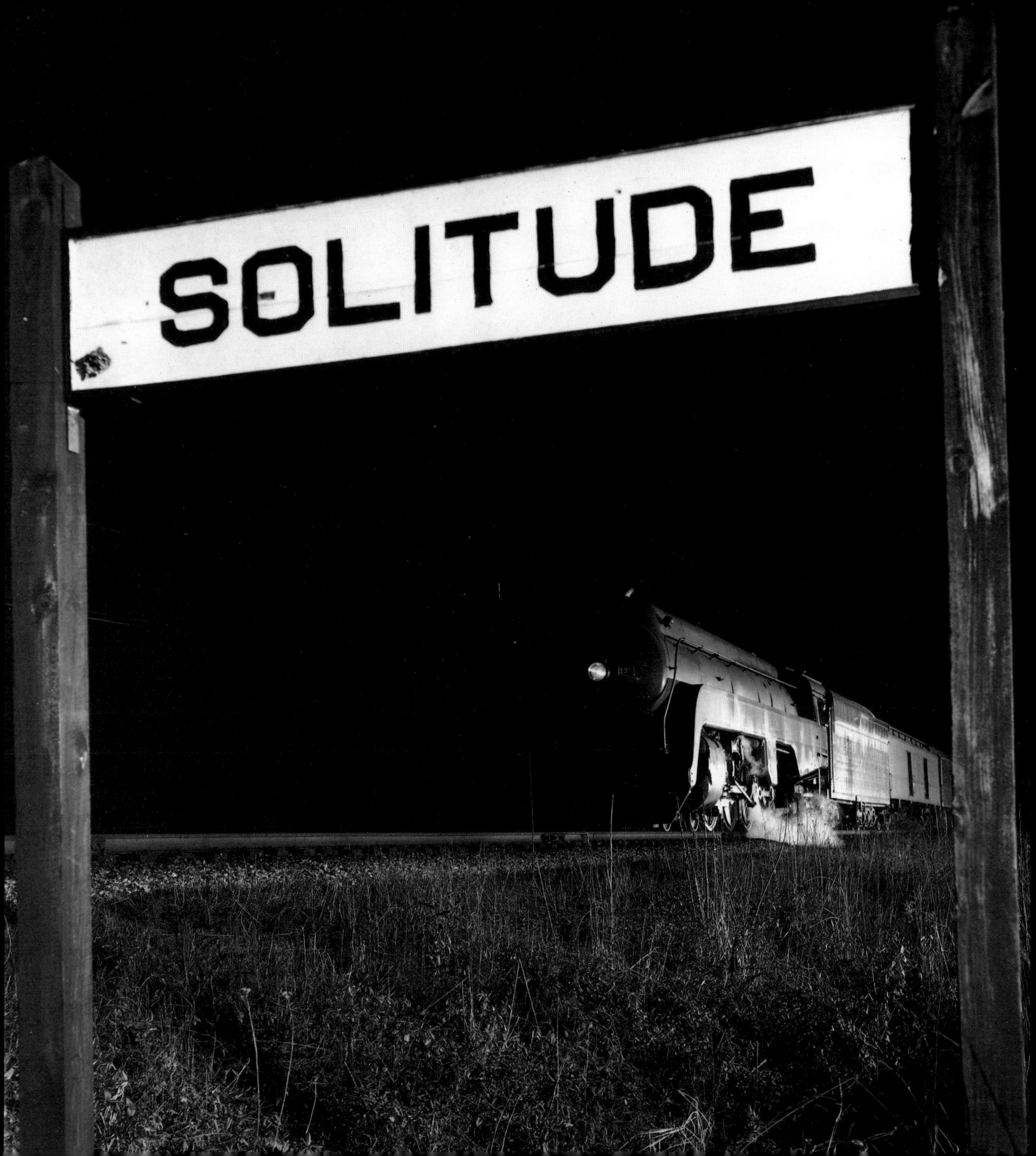
SOLITUDE

Backing past Hager Tower from the Western Maryland Roundhouse, where N&W passenger engines were serviced, K2a 130 moves to the Hagerstown Pennsy depot to take command of Train No. 1.

Above: Inside the Hager Tower, Operator Miller Ruth shows off the hand-thrown levers with which he makes his living.
Right: From the Hager Tower, Student Operator J. H. Shank, seated in the swivel chair, takes instruction from W. J. Smith, far right, in controlling trains from any of the three railroads that may enter the yard. Taking a break until they can go back to work are C. E. Nonemaker, a PRR section man, and J. E. Burke, a refugee from a halted Western Maryland yard engine.

Entering Luray, Virginia, from the south, time freight 96 crosses U.S. Highway 340 above Hawksbill Creek as Barry Good and five Judd siblings cool off on a summer night. The name of the children's hometown is derived from that of Lewis Ramey, an early settler.

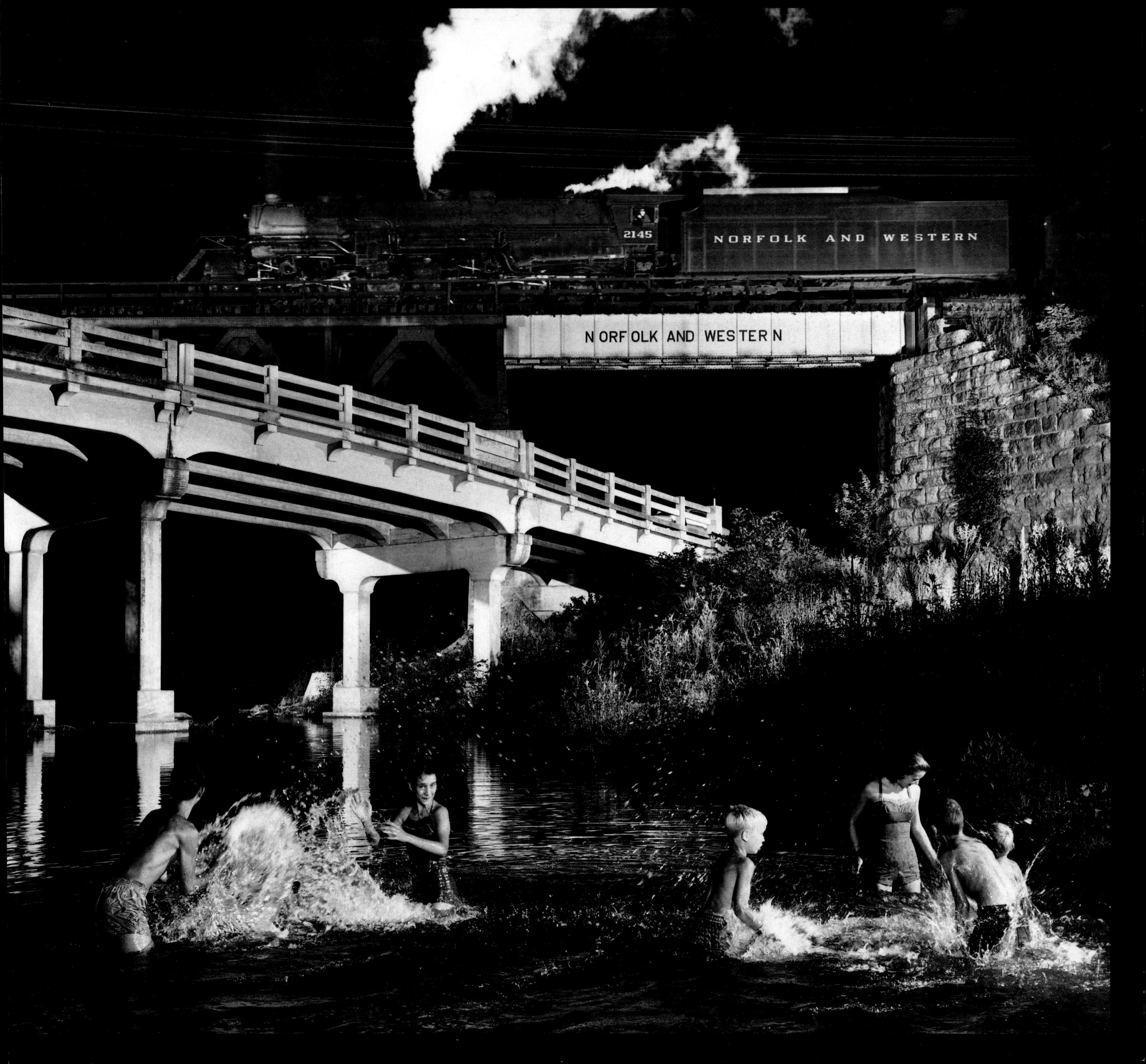
NORFOLK AND WESTERN
2145
NORFOLK AND WESTERN

At Luray, Second 51, a southbound time freight, crosses the Lee Highway, a north—south road that was popular before the advent of the Interstates.

Right: Policeman Weldon Painter patrols the main street of Stanley, Virginia, as First No. 51 south streams through the level crossing.
Overleaf, left: Y6 2120 roars through Luray at 3:00 A.M. on March 23, 1956. Photographer Link strung over a third of a mile of wire to set off 36 flash bulbs for this photograph, which took first place in the professional class of the 1957 Graflex International Photo contest.
Overleaf, right: By day, Luray Crossing Watchman Archie Stover inhabits the elevated shanty behind him, where he controls the flashers and gates during extended switching by a local freight on the town's industrial tracks.

Right: In the early hours of a foggy January morning, 1957, N&W No. 2, drawn by K2a 128, meets Baltimore and Ohio No. 7, the Chicago-bound *Shenandoah*, a train that has been diesel-powered for several years. Between the two railroads, this remote little transfer station once saw 36 passenger trains a day.

Below: Working as a relief agent-operator, George Beaghan takes charge of the station at Shenandoah Junction, West Virginia.

Scrambling to the summons of a train whistle that was presented to the town by the N&W for use as a fire siren, the Grottoes Volunteer Fire Department swings into action as Train Two scorches by.

W. A. Miller mans the old gravity-flow gas pump at the Vesuvius General Store, as No. 2 goes up the valley. Posing in Link's convertible are Bob Cullen and Jane Groah, who later married. Vesuvius was named for an iron furnace that operated there from 1828 to 1854.

Behind the counter of the Vesuvius store are the proprietors, Mr. and Mrs. Edgar Austin. Mr. Miller loafs beside the "Burnside No. 1" stove along with Thurston A. Graves, 84-year-old retired N&W agent, who served 57 years on the railway, having begun in 1888. Framed in the window is K2a 127 with Walter Finney as the engi-

First 51 south skirts past the Fitzgerald Lumber Company at Buena Vista, Virginia, in March 1956.

Above: Engine Watchman Bernie Cliff climbs atop the boiler of Class M2 1148 at Waynesboro to check the sand supply and to inspect the bell, whistle, and generator.

Left: To make this photograph of Train No. 2 going north beside the Gooseneck Dam of the Maury River, Winston Link spent four days in preparation, and had to string a rope bridge 150 feet over the water to transport his lighting equipment.

These two photographs of No. 2 on Bridge 425 at Arcadia were shot simultaneously from both sides of the bridge. The difficulty lay in keeping the lights on one side from interfering with the others. Steven Breeden shoos the cows as Walter Finney spurs K2a 129.

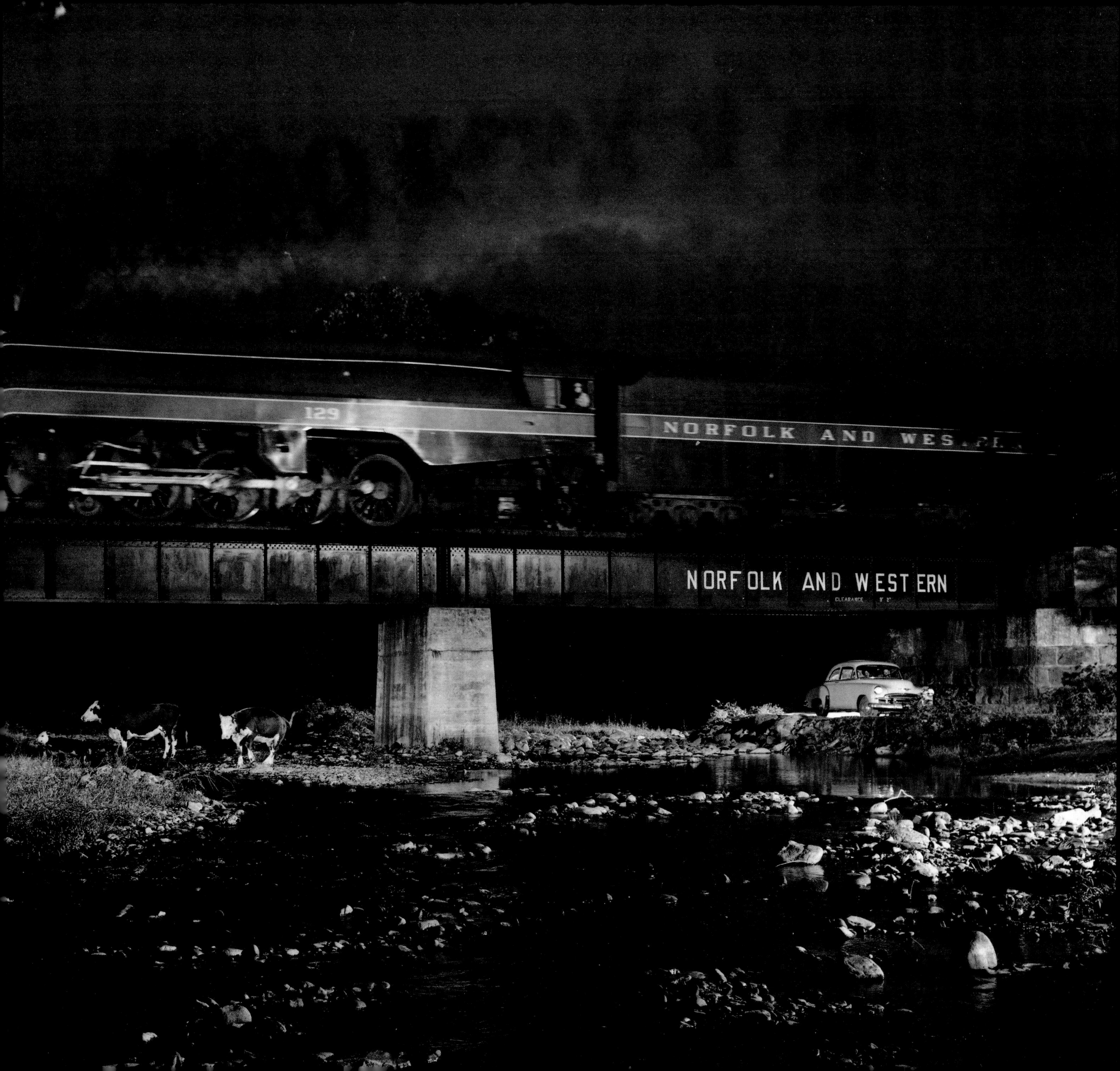
129
NORFOLK AND WESTERN
CLEARANCE

Preceding pages, left: Link and his assistant at the time, George Thom, decided at the last minute to photograph this cut at Lithia, Virginia, and struggled up a steep hill with a mountain of flash equipment. Once set up, their flash stopped Y6b 2175 in its tracks.
Preceding pages, right: After 48 years of tussling with N&W tracks, retired Section Foreman B. A. Fitzgerald (center) is content to watch the action from the front porch swing at the home of Mr. and Mrs. Charles W. Lugar, his Lithia neighbors. Train Two passes in the background of this July 31, 1955, scene.
Right: In the living room of Hester Fringer's home, a short distance south of Lithia, her grandson George Poulis observes his nightly ritual of waving to his railroader friends aboard No. 2 as his mother and the family pets enjoy the fireplace.

Below: Every evening, especially in the summer, N&W trains played a part in the easy-living style of the Shenandoah Valley. On the bridge across Back Creek leading to the Mungo Buchanan property at Lithia, the passing of this N&W locomotive doesn't disturb the Keith children's concentration as they try to hook a silvery-scaled specimen from the waters.

Right: Bobby Goggin, a small boy from a nearby farmhouse, tried unsuccessfully to get out of the way as Link shot this scene of a Y-Class locomotive shoving a northbound time freight by Fringer's Mill at Lithia, then a settlement of 101 souls in Botetourt County.

Right: On a 12-degree night in December 1955, James Harless gathers a few extra logs for the hearths of his 200-year-old cabin at Midvale, Virginia. In the background Y6b 2174 is about to cross State Route 714 with No. 96 north.

Overleaf, left: The "Lone Star Shifter," heading home from Roanoke, erupts after getting a "proceed" train order signal at Cloverdale. Members of the crew on February 8, 1957, were: L. R. Jones, engineer; G. W. Ralston, fireman; J. H. Gillespie, conductor; R. L. Talbert, head brakeman; and E. W. Janney, flagman.

Overleaf, right: Arriving at Natural Bridge "Station," as natives of the area say, Train No. 2 has just crossed over the James River and a C&O subdivision that extends from Clifton Forge to Richmond. Pictured are Frank Collins, Carl Tolley, and Phil Leighton.

On November 11, 1957, Winston Link received a letter from President Smith telling him that the Class J locomotives would be taken off the through Southern trains west of Lynchburg. Link wanted to get more pictures in the mountainous areas between Roanoke and Bristol, where the steam trains were integrally woven into the fabric of the people's lives.

What intrigued Link about the Radford Division was the beastly display of power the locomotives put on as they vaulted over the Alleghenies and plunged through several short tunnels to Walton. There, the double-track main line continued west along the New River to Bluefield and the single-track Bristol Line split off

4

Beauty and the Beast on the Radford Division

through an area rich in agriculture and history. Scattered along the line were ornate stations of William Mahone lineage, and at its end was a roundhouse where the engines could be photographed in their natural habitat.

Once known as the Pulaski Division, the Bristol Line became an important freight route as a member of the "Great Southern Despatch" fast freight partnership. As for its passenger

Left: Jerry Reed and Minnie Tate ignore the approach of the fast-stepping *Birmingham Special* at Max Meadows, population 700.

heritage, the Bristol Line was a link in the "Great Southern Mail Route" between the North Atlantic and Gulf states when that service began in 1858. In 1860 it became one of the first routes to have sleeping-car service, only a year after the idea was first tried in Illinois. When the Civil War broke out in 1861 the line hauled thousands of rebel troops from the Carolinas, Georgia, and Louisiana to the battlefields of Manassas, then took many of them back home on the first trainload of wounded evacuated from the carnage.

Memories of Link's last visit to the Bristol Line still bring a smile to his face. On the early morning of December 23, he was poised to shoot No. 18 at Max Meadows but backed off because the train came west beneath a plume of black smoke. After the train passed, Link used a special key to open a N&W phone box and asked the dispatcher if he could stop No. 18 and have it back up and come through again making white smoke. Although it was unheard of to stop a train for such a frivolous reason, the "train runner" gave his permission. After backing to about a mile east of Max Meadows, *The Birmingham Special* thundered ahead spewing a stack of white smoke as Link desired. But getting the photograph was small consolation, for steam operations on the Bristol Line ended on a sad New Year's Eve a week later.

Right: Train 18 roars through Max Meadows for the second time on the morning of December 23, 1957, after Link convinced the dispatcher to have it back up and return making white smoke.
Overleaf, left: Class A 1241 bursts from the westbound portal of the twin Montgomery Tunnels east of Christiansburg.
Overleaf, right: Train No. 17 crosses Bridge 201 just east of Wurno Siding, so named because before one was put up there "were no" sidings there.

Preceding pages, left: Norvel Ryan and son herd their cows for milking in December's early darkness near Shawsville, as No. 3, *The Pocahontas*, barrels by on its all-night run to Cincinnati. Preceding pages, right: Breaking a tradition of the Baumgardners, who represented the railroad here from 1857 to 1947, Agent J. L. Akers waves No. 17 through the station at Rural Retreat. Behind the depot is a drugstore where the soft drink Dr. Pepper was first concocted.

Right: A giant oak tree with a circumference of over 18 feet reaches out to embrace the westbound *Birmingham Special* at Max Meadows. Link was hoping to catch an owl in the branches, but lighting 360 feet of rail presented problems enough.

Left: Silent Night at Seven-Mile Ford during the Christmas season of 1957 finds the peace broken only by the passage of Class J 611 over Bridge 322. Fresh from cutting a yuletide tree are Charles Jackson, Sr. and Jr., along with the Johnson boys and Brownie.

Overleaf, left: From the porch of their Victorian home at Max Meadows, Mr. and Mrs. Ben Franklin Pope bid farewell to an old friend as Class J pulls the last steam train to Bristol on December 31, 1957. Ben Dulaney was aboard No. 17 that night.

Overleaf, right: Jane White and her brother Ben Dulaney leave the Presbyterian church at Seven-Mile Ford after services on December 29, 1957. Train 17 puffs by in the background.

Following pages, left: Spoofing a famous poster painted by J. A. Burch in 1875 to advertise Lake Shore and Michigan Southern's *The Fast Mail*, Terry Friend and Minnie Tate pose with Train 42.

Following pages, right: Cashier Greek Blackard worked well past banker's hours to pose with No. 42, a train on the N&W timetables since 1902. The town of Crockett, nothing but a sawmill and store, hardly seemed to warrant a bank.

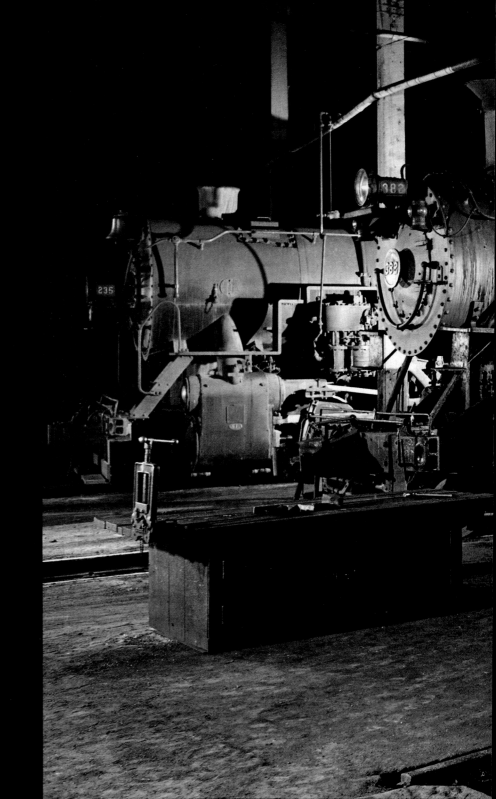

Preceding pages, left: Engine Supplyman T. A. "Andy" Smith sands K1 4-8-2 104, a 1916 product of Roanoke Shops, at the 16-stall Bristol roundhouse built in 1926.

Preceding pages, right: With the help of Night Roundhouse Foreman W. D. "Bill" Emmons at Bristol, Link was able to have the engines jockeyed about to his satisfaction. Here, a "hostler" (adapted to the iron horse from English stable keepers) positions the 104 for water as his helper tugs on the tank's lanyard.

Right: In Stall No. 1 of the Bristol Roundhouse, Class A Laborer J. H. Pope gives the grimy 104 a face lift as M 382 and S1a 235 wait for a washing.

Right: The 104 rides the Bristol "merry-go-round" as, in the background, Class J 606 leaves with the eastbound *Pelican,* known to old-timers as "The Vestibule." Link had to splice his cables to make this photograph after the wheels of the turntable cut the wires strung across the pit to his flash equipment.

Below: Posing proudly with the tools of their respective trades, Machinist O. N. Carroll and Hostler R. H. Carrier of the Bristol Roundhouse personify the spirit of the 21,000 loyal, conscientious employees dedicated to keeping the Norfolk and Western what they believed was America's best railroad.

Preceding pages, left: Once "Queen of the Fleet" before the Class J became N&W's premier passenger engine in 1941, K1 Mountain 104 lived out her last days on the Radford–Bristol local freight.
Preceding pages, right: In the days of steam a railroad's self-esteem could be judged by the luster of the brass on its engine bells. Here, Engine Cleaner R. E. Booher of the Bristol Roundhouse makes certain that N&W's house is in order.
Right: Ticket Clerk A. T. Moody is at work in the Bristol Union Station, a depot that the N&W shared, as it did all facilities at Bristol, with the Southern Railway.

Located deep in the mountains of Mingo County along the Kentucky border, Williamson, West Virginia, was a place whose very lifeblood was inextricably tied to the surrounding coal mines. Here, where the Scioto and Pocahontas divisions meet, the railway maintained the largest coal marshaling yards in the world, a roundhouse, and supporting shop facilities.

All night long lanterns of every color would wink throughout the vast assembly yards. Williamson's day officially began at 5:15 A.M. when the eastbound *Poca-hontas* rounded a bend and slipped into the passenger station. From that moment machin-ists, train crews, clerks, boiler-makers, carmen, section and round-house laborers,

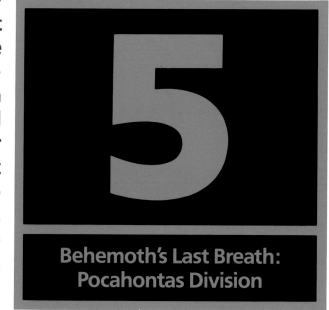

5

Behemoth's Last Breath: Pocahontas Division

and switchtenders would join ranks as they strode to their workplaces, eager to tamp ballast down at the east limits of the yard, tackle a faulty feedwater pump on that Class A just off No. 86 from Portsmouth, or send a Y6 up to Cinderella on the Sycamore Branch.

In Williamson a railroader received as much respect as, say, a judge, a minister, or a doctor.

Left: Pride in his craft is apparent as Engineer J. R. Harrell pauses at the Shaffers Crossing Roundhouse before leaving for Bluefield, West Virginia, headquarters of the Pocahontas and Western general divisions.

Little boys would gape in open-mouthed awe as their idols passed by. ("Look," they would whisper, nudging each other, "there goes Ole' Walter Carter. Why, he's the engineer on the *Pow'tan!*") Williamson. Dirty, filthy, gritty, N&W-born and bred, Williamson. Now *there* was a railroad town.

Fitting then that it be the last bastion of big-time steam railroading in the United States. The N&W was dieselizing faster than ever before, and the steam locomotive was driven back to a fortress of the very ingredient from which it derived its strength and owed its birth more than 150 years before. Finally, there was only one place where the hoot of a Y6 whistle would reverberate off the steep hills... Williamson. But nothing could prolong the life of the steam locomotive much longer.

Ben Dulaney told Winston Link late in April 1960 that if he wanted to do any more work, he'd better hurry. There were so many things that Link wanted to do before time ran out.

On the morning of May 6, 1960, Y6 2190 trundled the Pigeon Creek Shifter as far west as Kermit on the last main line run; later that afternoon, S1a 291 was called to work on a second trick yard job. It was in the wee hours of May 7, when a hostler sadly and lovingly eased the little 291 to a coupling with the 2190, that steam, and Link's project, died softly in the night.

Right: Engine Supplyman J. O. Haden, posing with an alemite gun at Bluefield in 1955, before the civil rights movement, never dreamed he could ever become a machinist when this picture was made.
Overleaf, left: Lubricator Charles Wade attends to the rods of Class E2a 578 at the lubritorium in Bluefield.
Overleaf, right: On this July 1955 night in Bluefield, Lubricator A. L. Poteet will complete his chores on the 563 in about 11 minutes.

These pages: Proud to be career railroad men are the N&W employees in these pictures, among them (upper left) Engineer A. B. "Buddy" Reynolds, who retired in 1959 after a spotless 53-year career; (lower left) Fireman R. A. Spradlin and Engineer J. W. Kitts; (opposite) Brakemen P. H. Dupuy, F. B. Gibson, and Clinton Fouch, Conductor Greg Preston, Fireman Joe E. Estes (between Gibson and Fouch), and standing in gangway, Engineer J. D. Linck.
Overleaf, left: Train 16, *The Cavalier*, leaves a rainy Williamson.
Overleaf, right: Great billows of steam from the roaring cylinder cocks of Y6b 2190 shroud Joe Estes on the Pigeon Creek Shifter.

Preceding pages, left: Running briskly on the main line west of Williamson, "Second Pigeon," a Kermit-bound mine run, backs through West Virginia coal country in March of 1960.
Preceding pages, right: On March 16, 1960, less than two months before the engine was retired, Y6b 2190's boiler would soon be as cold as the icicles at the Massey mine near Gilbert, West Virginia.
Right: Roaring through a tunnel of time, Y6 2136 charges toward Williamson in a stone-and-brick-lined bore at the city's west end. Link had asked for westward trains to be diverted over the eastbound track to set up his flash units for this shot.

The "Magnetic Flagman" wig-wag crossing signal begins its dizzy dance as a Y6b steams into Panther, West Virginia. The station at this remote place was one of the few on the line to have an agent's quarters upstairs.

This trackside swimming pool is located in Welch, West Virginia, the bustling county seat of the "Free State of McDowell." Things in Appalachia were not always as bad as the press made them out to be! Poolside, Anne Barnes, Nilda Ramella, and Vesta Kitchen flirt with Winston Link's nephew Corky Zider.

At the Iaeger Drive-In Theater Willie Allen and Dorothy Christian appear impervious to "Hot Shot" merchandise on the move. An A-Class engine like the eastbound 1242 was not usually operated over the Pocahontas Division, but when Time Freights 77–78 were inaugurated to run at near-passenger train speeds in 1955, they were assigned to the swift runs.

The orange rays of the late October sun are just beginning to peep over the ridges surrounding the tobacco-market town of Abingdon as the Norfolk and Western Train 201, the daily-except-Sunday mixed to West Jefferson, rattle-bangs to a stop in front of the faded, red-brick station. Pulling one coach, a baggage-mail, and several assorted freight cars, the ancient Class M locomotive, No. 382, celebrating her fiftieth anniversary in this year of 1956, casts a wavering silhouette against a nearby warehouse. The heat from the stack contrasts sharply with the cool mountain air.

6

All Aboard for the Virginia Creeper

Inside No. 201's coach, Conductor Ralph White ambles along, taking up tickets from the few riders inside. Under his arm he carries a carton of lollipops, for today the "candy man" makes his traditional appearance on the Abingdon Branch, a Saturday morning treat for all the youngsters living along the line.

Reeling his Hamilton from the deep pool of his pocket, the conductor notes that, at 7:40 A.M., the train is already ten minutes behind schedule. However, he assures all within hear-

Left: "Ole Maud" curtsies to her iron counterpart as the _Virginia Creeper_ struggles around a curve into Green Cove. This scene was not set up; the horse and dray just happened by, and photographer Link alertly took advantage of it.

ing distance, "we'll be on our way as soon as 'Honey Fitz' gets done with his whistle."

Up on the throbbing boiler of Engine 382, Engineer Fitzhugh Talmadge Nichols is making hurried adjustments to his custom-made "bootleg" quill, bolting the thin strands of a wire cable through the eye of a dangling, once limber lever, now rigid from the two-hundred-pound force of the steam. Satisfied that all is sound, he scoots along the running board and swings his stout figure through the door on the fireman's side. He vanishes around the backhead as a twist on the blower valve by the "fireboy" sends a billow of gray coal smoke into the blue sky. In a matter of seconds, two wisps of white steam from the musical pipes of the metal organ signal that the mixed is moving on.

With a gentle jolt, we are off on a journey back in time, promenading grandly through the pumpkin patches and the fodder-shocked fields of harvest. Around every bend of the fifty-five-and-a-half-mile route will be beauty to behold as the time-forgotten train breaks through the narrow gorges cut by cascading streams into sun-splashed meadows and furrowed farm-lands. In fact, on the way up to White Top, Virginia, and down to West Jefferson, North Carolina, the *Virginia Creeper*—affectionately named both for its slow speed and for the many varieties of ivy encountered along its way—will pass through some of the most spectacular scenery in the South.

The *Virginia Creeper* was a rare bird even to have lasted as it did into the second half of the twentieth century. Though the conception of the mixed train is as old as railroading itself, the evolution of the modern-day species can be traced to Depression-era economics more than anything else. There were other secondary-line mixed trains that made it into the mid-1950s on the Norfolk and Western, notably Nos. 111–112, the Virginia Tech taxi service between Christiansburg and Blacksburg known as the *Huckleberry*, and Nos. 311–312, the *Tri-State Limited*, on the Buchanan Branch from Devon, West Virginia, through a tip of Kentucky into Grundy, Virginia. None, however, could come anywhere near matching the country charms of a ride on the Abingdon.

More important to the isolated inhabitants of the mountains that hugged Trains 201 and 202, it was their main connection with the outside world, bringing them the basic necessities for daily living as well as mail-order notions from the Sears-Roebuck catalogue and letters from Aunt Levicy. They traveled the mixed to make application at the county courthouse for a marriage license, take a piano lesson, have a saw sharpened, or reach their favorite fishing holes. To them, the train was one of their own.

Chartered as the Abingdon Coal and Iron Railroad Co. in 1887, the line made little progress until, in 1898, it was reorganized as the Virginia-Carolina Railroad. By 1905 its owner, W. E. Mingea, had completed laying rail from Abingdon through Damascus to Konnarock, Virginia, a distance of almost thirty-one miles, in order to reach the fine Appalachian hardwood lumber that could be found there.

In 1912 the Norfolk and Western bought a

controlling interest in the property and financed a forty-nine-mile extension toward Elkland, North Carolina, from a place called Creek Junction. Two years later the construction was completed, giving the railroad a main line of almost eighty miles.

That same year, 1914, the remainder of the Mingea holdings, including 6 locomotives and 210 pieces of rolling stock, was also purchased. Thrown in with the deal was E. P. Kinzel, president and general manager, who was retained as train- and roadmaster after the N&W officially took over the subsidiary, to be known as the Abingdon Branch of its Radford Division, on August 27, 1919.

Originally there were both a dispatcher's office and an engine house at Abingdon, as business was brisk on the branch. In those days, Nos. 201–202 were operated as a regular four-car varnish run between Abingdon and West Jefferson (letting Nos. 213–214 handle the mixed-train duties all the way to Elkland, which was known as the "South End").

In addition to the passenger jobs, there were often as many as six freight trains a day, assisted by pusher engines stationed at White Top and West Jefferson. It was not unusual to see a doubleheader coming off the branch with forty or fifty cars, and it took all air and hand brakes, tied up with a spring pole by men with backbone and courage, to get safely down White Top Mountain.

Business declined when timber resources were exhausted and the Great Depression hit, and the runs both from West Jefferson to Elkland and from Abingdon to Konnarock were discontinued in 1933. After that, Nos. 201 and 202 were deemed sufficient to serve the needs of the "creeper" counties, and they were degraded to mixed-train status, making-up and terminating at Bristol and running to and from Abingdon as an extra. A single Class M locomotive could usually handle what livestock and lumber business that remained, augmented only occasionally by a car of copper ore, electrical components, gasoline, soapstone, or wood by-products.

At the insistence of Ben Dulaney, O. Winston Link first went down to take a look at the Abingdon Branch in June 1955. Before then he had been interested primarily in night photography. But the *Virginia Creeper* ran only during the daylight hours, and both Link and Dulaney realized the importance of capturing the line on film before it faded into extinction.

By the time Link became acquainted with it, the *Virginia Creeper's* lone coach was already often overflowing with "furriners," as the visiting outlanders were known, in the forms of railfans and tourists. They came from far and wide to ride the fabled train, particularly when the fall foliage was at its height of splendor.

But if the Abingdon Branch was a dream come true to the rail enthusiasts, to the N&W management it was rapidly becoming a nightmare. It was terribly expensive both to operate and to maintain.

Motive power on the line was limited to a Class M 4-8-0 (usually the 382, 396, or 429, all of which were outfitted with a heavily flanged spark-arrester stack to prevent fires from starting on the thick-forested right-of-way; the 495 was also used until it dropped its crown sheet near Damascus in 1953) or lighter, owing to the weight restrictions on the many bridges, most of which were built of heavy timber bents. With the Class M's maximum tractive effort of only 40,163 pounds, it was necessary to either doublehead or double the hill on the trip up to White Top if the train exceeded 325 tons (about 5 cars). And the return trip up the other side of the mountain was not much easier.

As for the bridges, there were 108 of them, in all makes and sizes; sharp curves, more than a hundred of them, were also a problem. Flash flooding provided a constant threat, and more than once the railroad rebuilt the branch after raging torrents tore out fills and trestles.

Pulling out of Abingdon, we leave the heavy-duty Walton–Bristol main line about half a mile north of the station, veering to the right as we slowly move out onto the much lighter rail of the *Virginia Creeper.* Gradually picking up speed, the train soon reaches the maximum allowable speed of twenty-five miles per hour, making its way through dense, undulating woodlands hemmed in by craggy cliffs and over several "dry bridges."

As our train passes over one of these spans, it spooks out from under it some cattle that had been using it for shelter. Frequently such cattle wander out onto the decks (their favorite seems to be Bridge Eight), and the crew, if they can stop the train short enough to avoid hitting the animals, must resort to diplomatic means to clear the way—especially if it is a bull handling the bovine end of the bargaining.

Once past Watauga, we break away from the high cliffs and steep drops into wide meadowlands. After a flag stop at Alvarado, little more than a country store and a church nestled around the tiny station house, we progress through the fields of Delmar, Drowning Ford, and Vails Mill. Along the way, the loud chime whistle sounds to clear the farmers' lanes.

At Damascus—population 1,726, a "city" by Abingdon Branch standards—we slow for our first scheduled stop. Shortly after the turn of the century, this community was an early rail center where connections were made with two short-lived lumber lines, the standard-gauge Beaver Dam Railroad (which tied into the Crandull & Shady Valley) and the narrow-gauge (thirty-six-inch) Laurel Railway. But as the lumber trade died off, so did the area's prosperity.

Conductor White goes up ahead to supervise the setting off of some gondolas for the purpose of loading logs, leaving Flagman J. M. "Scutch" Stevens in charge of the cut-off cars. Before he leaves, White cautions the flagman to keep a keen watch for any local boys who might try to finance a day's outing by hitching a ride, hobo-style, in an empty box car.

From Damascus to Creek Junction, the train flirts with the Tennessee border, playing a sort of leap frog with the restless water of White Top Creek, an excellent trout stream, which we will cross nineteen times in a little more than eleven miles. There are no passengers for either stream-side Laureldale or Taylors Valley (home of the only two-story station on the branch) today, although they are both favorite stops of tourists in the spring and summer because of their lush growth of rhododendron and mountain laurel.

Reaching Creek Junction, the train stops to drop off and pick up the mail for nearby Konnarock. The railroad once served as the center of the entire Creek Junction–Konnarock area, but about the only reminder left of those days is a decrepit, wooden, center-sill boxcar, once used

Engineer Joe McNew, shown reaching for the engine brake and watching for a brakeman's hand signals, was known to get every ounce of tractive effort a "Mollie" like the 429 could muster.

as a telegraph office but now lying abandoned, its walls mostly missing, the wood having been used for kindling by local fishermen.

The engineer takes this opportunity to refill the tender with water from an old, tuscan-colored, wooden tank. The methodical sound of steel clanging against steel can be heard ringing above the gurgling waters, as the fireman attempts to blow up a good head of steam. Though we have been climbing steadily since Alvarado, we are now about to start up the even steeper slopes of White Top Mountain, which will demand every ounce of fortitude and skill that the "Mollie" (as the Class Ms are dubbed by the engine crews) and the men in her cab can muster.

The increase in altitude is readily apparent climbing out of the Junction, as the water-level road to Konnarock, to the right of the tracks, seems to drop. A mile farther south the incline becomes even more noticeable as we bridge Green Cove Creek, suddenly far below us.

The exhausts of the engine are coming slower and slower now as it leans into the grade of White Top Mountain. On both flanks of the mountain, the speed limit has been reduced to eighteen miles per hour, but we do not even approach that speed. The *Virginia Creeper* slows to a crawl, very much in danger of stalling.

Just when it seems as if the twelve-wheeler is about to bog down, a long blast of the meadowlark whistle signals a two-hundred-yard stretch of level land, and we ease to a stop at Green Cove station.

On the cinder platform in front of the white

and green-trimmed depot stands a bespectacled gentleman clad in a khaki work suit held together by suspenders. His balding pate is hidden beneath a black uniform cap, with a brass badge above the bill that identifies him as "a-g-e-n-t." This is Mr. W. M. Buchanan, who, in addition to being the railway's representative here, also holds the Western Union franchise and is postmaster and proprietor of a small store, all of which are housed under the station's roof.

Anyone can see that the picturesque depot was the central gathering place in the tiny hamlet of Green Cove, but its importance is best related by Mrs. Anne Gentry, who grew up here. (Like so many other residents of the Appalachian region, she and her husband had to leave the economically depressed area for the more prosperous industrial cities of the North.)

"In the mornings we'd get up and wait for the train to come in," Mrs. Gentry fondly recalls. "After it was gone, we'd peek through the pigeon holes in the corner that was the post office, watching Mr. Buchanan stamp all the letters and waiting to see if we got any mail.

"Everybody came and visited. We sat out on the freight landing in the summertime and inside around the stove in the winter.

"There was no electricity up here for most folks back then. We'd bring a gallon container and Mr. Buchanan would go back in the ware-room and fill it with lamp oil out of a barrel for ten cents."

Mr. Buchanan's wife, Mary, and daughters, Adele and Eleanor, also helped to supplement the family's income. Back in the days when the passenger train was well-patronized, they sold from fifty to seventy-five box lunches a day at fifty cents a box.

Highlights of the pre-packaged meals (which were ordered from Abingdon or Damascus by wire) were Mrs. Buchanan's fried chicken, country ham sandwiches, home-baked biscuits, and fresh fruit tarts. The entire family arose every morning at three o'clock to have everything ready for the *Virginia Creeper* passengers. The Buchanans raised the chickens and hogs, plucked the feathers, and processed the hams all on their Green Cove property.

Whenever there was a special train on the branch the officials riding it would always stop off for lunch with the Buchanans. "I've had old R. H. Smith's knees under my table many a time," Mrs. Buchanan was proud of saying. But it wasn't just the Buchanans' cooking that brought them the respect and affection of the community. Mr. Buchanan was the mainstay of this beautiful rural area, and he was quick to donate food and shelter to all who came to him in need—no questions asked.

Soon the train's work at Green Cove is completed. In the comforts of our friendly visit it was easy to ignore the arduous journey that lies ahead, but from here to White Top we will be challenged by a sustained 3 percent gradient for a distance of two-and-a-half miles. As the crow flies the distance between the stations is only a mile, but the rough terrain necessitates a three-mile route by rail, so we circle and climb around the Abingdon Branch version of "Horseshoe Curve."

Getting out of Green Cove, the flanges of the steel wheels scream in pinched protest as the 382 swings around the too-tight bend a mile beyond the station. Fighting hard to hold the slippery rails—made even more slippery by the fallen leaves—the straining engine marches to the steady beat of its own exhausts.

Pistons pounding back and forth in their cylinders, the old Class M lunges into a final left-hand curve. With its safety valve shouting in triumph the 4-8-0 coasts to a stop at the White Top station. Directly ahead is the summit of the White Top grade. The station's altitude of 3,585 feet makes it the highest point attained by a passenger train east of the Rockies and the highest on a common carrier for a standard-gauge railroad anywhere in the country.

From the station platform we are afforded a superb view of the cloud-kissed cap of White Top Mountain, at 5,520 feet second only to Mt. Rogers as the highest point in Virginia. A cover of wild grasses that assume a white color when they die out and snow on its peak combine to give White Top Mountain the albino appearance from which it takes its name.

The serenity of the scene can be misleading, however, for the mood of the mountain can turn ugly with blizzards and biting winds in a matter of minutes. Section Man William V. Surber recalls having to chop ice off the water tank at Green Cove every day in the cold months in order to thaw the gravity pipes of the spout. A Virginia-Carolina passenger train once became snowbound on the Horseshoe Curve during the winter of 1917–18, its occupants having to take refuge in the Buchanans' house until a relief train got through the storm.

It was during one of those bleak times, however, that the Abingdon Branch had perhaps its finest moment. Every day for the two weeks prior to March 5, 1942, snow had been piling up around the mountains of Grayson County, Virginia. Inside a little cabin, five thousand feet up and five miles away from the N&W station at White Top, Mrs. Wade W. Weaver lay critically ill. She had gone into labor early that morning, expecting the birth of her sixth child. (It was not unusual for babies to be born at home in the mountains, often with only a midwife or "granny woman" in attendance.) Realizing that his wife was having difficulty with the delivery, Mr. Weaver put a phone call through to Dr. Rex Legard in Damascus. The physician and his nurse, Sister Sophia Moeller, quickly boarded Train 201 for White Top. Upon reaching their snowy destination, they found the trails that posed as roads impassable, with heavily crusted drifts as high as fifteen feet. They tried to plow their way through with borrowed horses, but their mounts soon bogged down, and they were left to struggle the rest of the way on foot.

Upon examining Mrs. Weaver, Dr. Legard determined that she must be taken to a hospital at once. The more immediate problem, though, was getting her back to the White Top station in time to catch the No. 202, about to depart for Abingdon, forty-five miles away and the site of the nearest medical facility. How could they possibly make it before the train pulled out?

It didn't take long to decide. Dr. Legard made a frantic phone call to Mrs. Gladys Harriger, the agent at White Top (one of only four women to hold that position for the N&W). Without hesitation Mrs. Harriger agreed to hold the train, which was at that very moment standing at her station ready to leave. Never mind that Mr. Weaver was her brother; she would have held the train anyway.

Now at least there was hope. Mrs. Weaver was bundled in warm blankets and placed on a mattress fastened to a two-horse sled. Stumbling down the mountain paths, horses, husband, doctor, nurse, and a few hastily summoned relatives accompanied her on a perilous journey.

Before the pitiful caravan made much progress, the snorting horses stomped through the crusts of ice and tumbled down, unable to continue. Men took their places, as neighbors grabbed up the traces and forced the sled onward. By the time they reached White Top nearly fifty men, women, and children had joined the mountain-style mission of mercy.

Finally, after an ordeal of almost three hours, they saw the train—still waiting! Quickly, trainmen made the transfer through a coach window and Engineer Ben Ball started Class M No. 429 rolling down the mountainside, battling the blockades of snow that were piled half-way up the sides of the cab. Swiftly but safely the train made a nonstop run to Abingdon, where it was met by an ambulance, ready to relay Mrs. Weaver on the last leg of the desperate race.

At the George Ben Johnson Memorial Hospital everything had been prepared (Conductor J. F. Anderson had wired ahead), and one of the quickest Caesarian operations on record was performed. Happily, the result of these frenzied efforts was a healthy, blue-eyed, brown-haired, seven-pound baby boy. The baby's name? Why Richard *Norwest* Weaver, of course!

Our stay at White Top completed, it is now time to continue on our journey. Slowly the *Virginia Creeper* pulls out of the station, edges its way over the crest, and begins to ramble down the other, "yon side" of the mountain on a roller-coaster ride into North Carolina.

Blue smoke issues from chafing brakeshoes now as Engineer Nichols keeps our consist in check with a minimum reduction of the automatic or "big" air. He takes these extra precautions against derailments here because of the severe weight restrictions on the bridges—even the miniature Wreck Car kept at Bristol is not allowed on this branch line.

The first town we reach in the "Tar Heel State" is Nella, near the bottom of the grade. Actually, the town is known by that name only in the pages of the N&W timetables; originally it was called "Allen," but the riders often confused it with Alvarado, so the spelling of its name was simply reversed. To further add to the confusion, the inhabitants of the hollow refer to it as "Husk." Whatever its name, it is marked only by a general store whose siding is peppered with signs, and by Jimbo, the Heinz-57 "Hound of Husk" that keeps guard over it.

Approaching Tuckerdale, the country begins to open up into farmland again. Our next stop is Lansing, where lunch for the crew is handed on from a cafe near the station. (The trays, with payment left on them, will be taken back on the return trip.)

There is no business at Bina today, so we go on to Warrensville, skirting along the headwaters of the New River, crossing its north fork before we roll into town. We drop off a few passengers here, then head on to the next stop—Smethport. There is no need to stop in Smethport, so we go right on to West Jefferson, the end of the line, grinding to a halt in front of the depot in this farming center—population 871—which also offers some fine home-cooked meals in restaurants on the town square.

At Creek Junction the delivery of the U.S. mail is held up a bit for a report on how the trout are hitting at a local fishing hole. The boxcar, formerly a telegraph office, was torn up for firewood.

There is a half-hour layover in West Jefferson as the crew prepare for the return trip. They turn the locomotive around on the wye and take water. Then they do considerable switching on a team track crammed with cars awaiting the offerings from local auction markets—mostly green beans, livestock, and tobacco.

The making-up of our train gives us the opportunity to "take spot" with some of the railmen as they reminisce about some railroaders of bygone days. The Abingdon Branch has enjoyed more than its fair share of "characters" through the years, especially among the engineers. One early throttle jerker of note was "Uncle Billy" Thompson, who was always on the lookout for a manufacturer who could fashion an umbrella large enough to cover his superheated Class W 2-8-0; Smith Spears insisted that the only fault of *his* trim locomotive, a little V-class 4-6-0 951, was that it ran so fast it didn't give him time enough to wave at the ladies.

One of the most eccentric characters of all, however, would have to be J. B. "Joe" McNew, the senior engineman on the branch. In his early years he was known to have no mercy on an engine, always running with the throttle wide open and the reverse bar "down in the corner on sand"—whether going uphill or down!

Ted Berry, retired Roanoke Terminal road foreman of engines, recalls what it was like to fire for Joe McNew: "You couldn't keep coal on the grates. He'd beat one of those little Class Ms to death. I even saw him burn up an air pump one time, much less what he'd do to the valve

135

gear and frame each and every day."

After McNew retired in 1956, Engineer Nichols took over the Abingdon Branch run. Like so many railroaders whose names were buried in the back pages of the seniority list, he had been "forced away" from his home terminal at Bristol for many years. He was running the *Powhatan Arrow* between Roanoke and Bluefield when the opportunity to "mark up" on the *Virginia Creeper* came.

Nichols, who had started his career wiping engines at Norton on the Clinch Valley line, won his real fame as originator of the *Virginia Creeper's* distinctive-sounding chime whistle. To make Nichol's whistle chime so mellowly, Gang Foreman W. M. Richardson, of the locomotive department at Bluefield, took a regular N&W freight whistle and welded three ports of various lengths into the barrel, or bell, as it is properly called.

The new whistle was an immediate hit with the railfans and the residents along the line, one of whom claimed it would "make your shirttail fly up your back." Another stated simply that it was "the most goose-bumpy" whistle he had ever heard.

"People told me you could hear it farther than a regular whistle," Engineer Nichols beams. "A fellow who lived away up on Holston River about six miles told me his little boy would sit out on the front porch every morning and listen for me to come into Damascus."

The opinion of the people who lived along the branch line was very important to the railmen, who, in the words of Nichols, "tried every

way we could to accommodate 'em. We'd let 'em off and pick 'em up about anywhere they wanted." And the respect was certainly reciprocated; Nichols also tells stories of "natives" having cleaned the tracks of debris after severe storms.

The layover completed, the *Virginia Creeper* begins its trip back to Abingdon. Since most of the train's work was done on the way out, the scheduled running time on the return trip is twenty minutes shorter. Having less work for himself and his crew, Conductor White is free to

The "candy man," Conductor Ralph White, opens up his "office" to catch up on some of his paperwork on the return trip, when things on the *Virginia Creeper* are not so hectic.

retire to his "office" (actually two facing seats in the coach) to catch up on some paperwork.

At closely spaced intervals "Candy Man" White reaches into the box of lollipops beside him and goes back to the open service door of the baggage and mail car, now the last of the train, behind the coach. Along the way barefooted children beat a path trackside, hiding the candy they already received behind their backs and begging for some more goodies to come sailing their way. But they can't fool the conductor, for he knows who each of them is and where he or she lives.

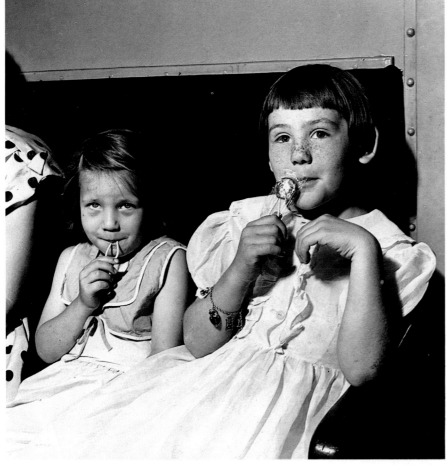

Young girls on the *Virginia Creeper* enjoy their "Saturday morning treat," courtesy of Conductor White, who also shares his lollipops with children who run trackside to the train.

Northward from Tuckerdale, the rails rise up steadily for ten and a half miles to White Top. The steep gradient makes it still a tough climb, but not as bad as it was on the southward trip. After a regular stop at Damascus and getting flagged down again at Alvarado, the train rolls into Abingdon right on schedule at 3:10 P.M.

All passengers are normally discharged here, where they can make connections with No. 45 into Bristol. But we are invited by Conductor White to ride on into Bristol with him, so that we can fully experience every phase of the mixed's operation.

From Abingdon to Bristol, though again running as an extra, Train 202 is handled just like a regular passenger train, right down into Union Station. There the crew is relieved of duty. The hostler and his "helper" (the switchman who "follows" him) detach the locomotive and take it to the roundhouse, where it will be serviced on the third shift. If the mixed were late, which is often the case, the dispatcher might let it come in as little as one block ahead of the *Tennessean*, though much to the dismay of the roundhouse General Foreman Emmons, who knows that this 1906-vintage engine was not built to outrun a Class J locomotive.

Later that night, we relax around the roundhouse office for a while, reflecting upon the fine day we just spent. Outside, the 382 is astraddle the turntable, being put to bed in a stall of the "barn," while the 429 awaits its turn to be tucked in. Tomorrow, Sunday, they'll rest. Come Monday, they'll have at it again with White Top Mountain.

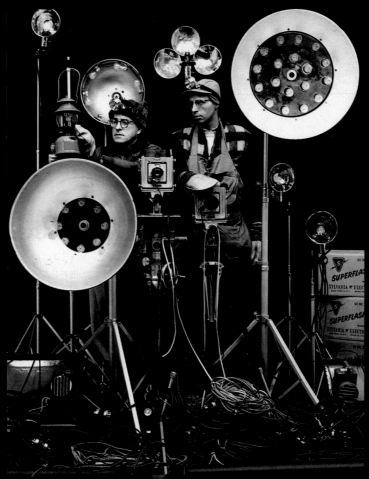

I worked for Winston Link for just over a year, from mid-1957 through the summer of 1958. I was studying in New York and was Winston's part-time assistant, hauling equipment, running out for props or supplies, and printing photographs in the darkroom. I made three trips with him to the Norfolk and Western that year, spending about a month along the line, and I learned a lot. Winston was a good teacher.

Winston was a successful commercial photographer of the old school, specializing in what was then called "industrial photography." He was exceptionally demanding, both on himself as a photographer and on his clients, too, for he required a free rein to develop his ideas, although he always remained remarkably sensitive to their needs. The studio was small, just Winston and one or perhaps two part-time assistants. He kept the overhead low so that he

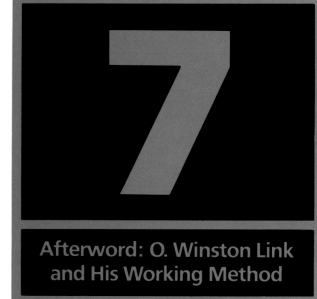

7

Afterword: O. Winston Link and His Working Method

Left: Throughout the five years that Winston Link documented the Norfolk and Western Railway he made thousands of photographs, each one demanding incredibly complex—and often dangerous—setups as well as hours of waiting time. These pictures show but a few of the difficulties Link overcame in order to position his cameras and banks of flashbulbs to go off at the precise instant necessary to freeze the scene and capture the full drama and magic of steam and steel beneath the stars. The picture in the middle of the bottom row shows Link and a former assistant, George Thom, setting up amid some of the equipment they brought with them.

could remain flexible in his assignments, taking those he wanted and rejecting the others, allowing him to devote himself to projects that demanded his love in addition to his intelligence and technical skills as a first-rate photographer.

The Norfolk and Western was the largest of these all-consuming, yet noncommercial projects that he undertook as a labor of passion and belief—but not the only one. Some day those images may appear to a wider public, much as the bulk of this Norfolk and Western work of some thirty years ago is only now being seen for the first time.

One could always tell when Winston was getting ready to go down to Virginia. Several big jobs would have been completed, the checks received and deposited, and time blocked out on the schedule. If we were making daytime photographs only, all the equipment could be contained in his 1952 Buick convertible, which Winston had purchased complete with a theoretically unavailable stick shift and a confidential factory service manual.

The leather back seat came out the day after he bought the car, replaced with a wooden platform to carry equipment. Winston rarely put the top down when driving but always put it down for ease in loading or unloading, his chief reason for always owning convertibles (station wagons were "too obvious"). His equipment on these trips would consist of two or three 4 x 5 Graphic view cameras with a number of lenses of different focal lengths, a Rolleiflex for fun, plenty of film, film holders, tripods, and often portable tanks and chemicals for processing the sheet film on the spot to check the results.

All this equipment filled up the trunk and back of the car. If night photographs were to be shot, we would hitch a trailer to the Buick. The flash equipment had been developed over a long period, and Winston, with an encyclopedic knowledge of New York suppliers (and an equal knowledge of all their excuses) had had special reflectors spun of aluminum to accommodate from one to eighteen flashbulbs each. The units were snuggled into special cases of gray fiberboard made to fit.

Winston's first photographs of the Norfolk and Western had been largely taken during the day, but he wanted a drama and mystery that could only be achieved at night. Using his professional experience, Winston determined that portable, compact equipment could be built to light large-scale scenes instantaneously, freezing all motion. At first he attempted to operate the flash systems with electric eyes or radio controls, but these proved unreliable; his final lighting system was hooked together with wire, and we carried more than half a mile of it in the trailer.

Winston was never happier than when we pulled away from his studio on East 34th Street and headed south. We bypassed the proliferating franchise motels when we could, for Winston had a passion for the usable past—old buildings, old towns, old objects. He loved those things that were well and thoughtfully made and were mellow with use—in an era when nineteenth-century objects and buildings were regarded as failures of Victorian design.

On the trip down, Winston mixed talk of specific photographs he hoped to make with extended comparisons between the qualities of the past—honesty of manufacture, pursuit of simple pastimes—and the knock-off trash and jaded pleasures of the present day. Fortunately, Winston's outrageous sense of humor, one of his most sustaining sensibilities, would overpower his invective. The basic absurdity of one of his more horrific comparisons of "then and now" would overwhelm him, and he would bellow forth the "Winston laugh," half bark, half machine-gun fire, rising and falling, on and on, a laugh that has frequently turned the heads in an entire restaurant.

There were two areas in which the past did not obtrude: his respect for the current technology of his medium, and food. Winston never hesitated to purchase a piece of photographic equipment if he felt it might improve his results, and he was always experimenting with the latest films and processes. Such experiments were never carried out on the job, but were gradually introduced into his professional operation only after Winston had proved them to be of direct benefit to his work. Regarding the latter subject, food, it was difficult to eat well, or even indifferently, in many of the small coal-mining towns in which we spent a good deal of time. We often detoured to eat at Howard Johnson's restaurants—better then—where Winston introduced me to one of his favorite dishes, hot fudge sundaes made with peppermint-stick ice cream, to which I remain addicted today.

When we arrived at our destination, whether it was the Martha Washington Hotel in Abingdon, or any of a dozen other hotels or motels along the line, Winston was already well-known, not just because he had stayed there previously but because his mission was so particular to the local citizenry. In many of the coal towns the tracks of the N&W were jammed into the narrow valleys, fighting for space with the river, the main street of the town (which often doubled as the railroad right-of-way), and the houses and businesses as well. To the residents, the railroad was a constant. It was necessary to life, but it was obtrusive too, noisy and dirty. Visitors from big cities were also rare in that part of the country in the mid-1950s—this was much before the political and social fascination with Appalachia—and the arrival of this man in his Buick convertible filled with arcane equipment was a real public occurrence.

If night photographs were to be made, Winston had to assemble a small local crew to assist him, and, if there were to be people in the shots, recruit a cast, too. Townspeople were asked to go swimming in the nearby creek—and to splash vigorously, please, as the train went by. Once Winston offered to take a young couple to the drive-in movie as his guests if they would sit in his convertible and cuddle a bit as a Y6 thundered by, and he made from this scene one of his most memorable photographs. Folks almost always responded warmly to Winston, no matter how puzzled they might be by his request to photograph their cows as foreground objects to a train or to let him monopolize their porches or front rooms for a few hours in order to photograph them having a good time while a locomotive roared past outside. He was an event, and there were few events in those small towns then.

The planning of a photograph was a deliberate procedure for Winston Link. He would load 4 x 5 view cameras with both color and black-and-white film for daytime photographs and black-and-white exclusively for night shots. Quite possibly he had noted a potential location on a previous trip, at which time he would have made a little sketch, either in a special N&W notebook he always kept on these trips or in one of the series of consecutively numbered notebooks he has carried with him (and preserved) for more than thirty years. In yet another notebook, a special one prepared for nighttime photographs, Winston had calculated the power and throw of his flash reflectors equipped with different flashbulbs. On returning to the photo site, he would take precise measurements and determine where to place the flash equipment. Broad areas of light were often less a problem to create than those special spots of illumination—a boy's lantern or a light in a window—that had to be produced with individual flashbulbs.

The heart of Winston's flash system was the "red box," the power supply that fired all the flashbulbs and the cameras in a single, gigantic surge of power. He designed the system himself, a forerunner of the battery capacitor flash units just then becoming popular. Like World War II bombardiers with their Norden bomb-

sights, we never let the power supply out of our sight. About the size of a small makeup case and painted a dull red, it contained three separate battery capacitor power units capable of firing all the flashbulbs—up to sixty of them—simultaneously with the triggering solenoids on three view cameras. The unit was lightweight and spring-mounted in its box and was complete with circuits that could check the continuity of the flash hookup to make sure that no breaks had occurred in the line. After the photographs were set up, breaks in the line were frequently a problem, because the wires often stretched across streets, fields, or even rivers, as well as around or through buildings.

Setting up was hard work. The flash units were set approximately in place and assembled. Wires were snaked from them to the "red box," often making long detours to avoid obstructions. Sometimes they were not attached to the power source until the very last possible minute. Although the photograph might have been blocked out in Winston's mind months before, he was constantly making small refinements. Once Winston planned a night photograph in downtown Northfork, West Virginia, where the trains shared the narrow main street with automobile and pedestrian traffic. We set up in daylight, but as Winston studied the scene, he realized that something extra was necessary. The black locomotive and cars against the dark buildings needed a highlight, a sparkle—a light in the window. Without hesitation he knocked on the door of an anonymous third-floor apartment and surprised the nonplussed tenants with his request to plant a flashbulb—to go off in a few hours' time—in their living room. Such requests were rarely declined, and so in this case wires for the bulb were strung out of the room, along a hallway, down a flight of outside stairs, across the street, and finally across the tracks. The line would be severed by the leading wheels of the locomotive a second after the photograph was made.

Winston's sense of composition was so sure that he was able to arrange his photographs without their chief subject—the locomotive and train. Focusing, however, was another matter. Inexplicably, the same subject required different focus settings in daylight and darkness. During the day, he marked the point where he wanted the locomotive to be when he fired the cameras. Then, after dark, he would place an electric lantern on the spot, its lens partially covered with black tape, creating alternate stripes of light and dark, to mark the spot and create a convenient focusing target as well.

With the setup complete, waiting for the train was both tedious and difficult. The N&W maintained a good on-time schedule for its passenger trains, but freight trains were another story. Heavy freights hauling coal were the most common on the line, and their arrival was unpredictable. The wait could be nerveracking. We spent the time retesting circuits and trying to keep local residents out of camera range while at the same time attempting to appease their curiosity about how, and most interestingly, *why* such pictures were being made.

In answering "why," the explanation was often easier if it was prefaced by the remark that "the photographer is from New York City." New York, to those mountain folks, was a complete puzzlement; they knew only that people with strange pursuits lived there. But Winston, his unusual behavior in wanting to photograph this mechanical intrusion into their valleys notwithstanding, won them over. It was obvious that he not only cared about the work he was doing, but also about the special qualities of these people and their places as well. Winston liked them as individuals—survivors of a hard life, quirky and filled with stories. They loved to talk and Winston loved to listen.

Winston, his New York background aside, fit in well with these folks. He loved the local speech, and it was a wonderful counterpoint to listen to his hard Brooklyn accent followed by the soft mountain reply. I recall his once working with a young man who was helping with a night shot. The man was stringing wire, and, uncomfortable with the word "connections," he immediately shortened it to "neckshuns." For Winston Link, it's been "neckshuns" ever since.

Finally, after what might be hours of waiting, we would hear that sound, the far-off, minor-key note of the A or the Y6 whistle, melancholy and soft at that distance, but of indelible power, echoing in the valley. This was it. With the headlight piercing the blackness down the line, final connections were made and the townsfolk positioned or politely asked to move. The sound, the light, the incredible physical presence, thousands of tons of metal steadily, slowly moving toward us, was for me a mechanically sublime experience. In the last two hundred yards or so there would be an immense crescendo, but within that cacaphony of sound the animistic soul of a steam locomotive could be picked out: the high speed hiss and buss of the turbine generator for the locomotive's electric lighting, the clank of the connecting rods as they revolved around the drive wheels' crank pins, the grating roar of the steam-driven stoker, the throaty gargle of the feed water injector, and the subsonic rumble of those great wheels bearing upon the rails. Then would come the flash, almost equally imposing in its presence, but absolutely silent. We would stand transfixed. Time had all but stopped.

There was one spot I particularly remember, a small bridge that crossed the Blue Ridge grade just west of the summit. Looking down, west toward Roanoke, one could see the tracks for some distance, curving first slightly south, then north to disappear behind a hill. They skirted a small valley that fell away to the south. I recall reflecting on just what we were doing when we were there at twilight one evening. I compared Winston and myself to zoologists or anthropologists who work methodically to document a soon-to-be extinct species or aboriginal tribe undergoing such alteration by its contact with "civilization" that its own customs were destined to be obliterated without reprieve. What we documented of this area would be *the* record. No matter how indifferent our society might be to our endeavors at the time, I knew that someday there would be interest in and respect for what Winston was preserving in such a thoughtful and visually powerful way.

Then we heard that sound, and we could only watch. First we saw the smoke blowing across the valley from behind the hill. Moments later the headlight spotted the gloom, and we felt rather than heard the slowly growing energy of two huge locomotives, physically alive in the sounds of their labors, inching thirteen thousand tons of coal and steel over the hill—before the noise and the smell took over.

Those moments of waiting made us sensitive to every nuance of these places, not simply to the sights and sounds of the soon-to-vanish steam locomotives, but to the landscape around us, beautiful in its natural state, and to the strong, straightforward, plain, and honest folks who populated it. I knew that the machinery we were documenting would never return, but I was not aware then that thirty years would so completely transform the towns and their people. Somehow in my mind they had become a fixed quantity.

It has taken the distance of thirty years, too, to begin to fully realize the impact of Winston Link's work. As we can now see, the romantic documentation of the vanishing machinery I thought was our sole purpose was only a fragment of his project's final meaning. For what Winston has preserved may now be seen as a wonderful and much more complex vignette of the individual lives of small-town America, and that, too, has all but vanished.

Thomas H. Garver
Madison, Wisconsin

144

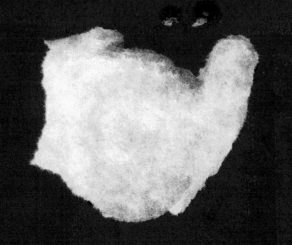